A Preparatory Redemption

The Proceedings of the Mormon Theology Seminar series is based on a novel idea: that Mormons do theology. Doing theology is different from weighing history or deciding doctrine. Theology speculates. It experiments with questions and advances hypotheses. It tests new angles and pulls loose threads.

The Mormon Theology Seminar organizes interdisciplinary, collaborative, theological readings of Latter-day Saint scripture. Seminar participants with diverse backgrounds closely explore familiar texts in creative ways. In partnership with the Laura F. Willes Center for Book of Mormon Studies at the Neal A. Maxwell Institute for Religious Scholarship, the Mormon Theology Seminar presents these experiments upon the word to foster greater theological engagement with basic Mormon texts.

Series Editor
Brian M. Hauglid

Other Mormon Theology Seminar *books include:*

Adam S. Miller, ed.,
An Experiment on the Word: Reading Alma 32

Joseph M. Spencer and Jenny Webb, eds.,
Reading Nephi Reading Isaiah: 2 Nephi 26–27

Julie M. Smith, ed.,
Apocalypse: Reading Revelation 21–22

Jeremiah John and Joseph M. Spencer, eds.,
Embracing the Law: Reading Doctrine and Covenants 42

Adam S. Miller, ed.,
Fleeing the Garden: Reading Genesis 2–3

Adam S. Miller, ed.,
A Dream, a Rock, and a Pillar of Fire: Reading 1 Nephi 1

Adam S. Miller and Joseph M. Spencer, eds.,
Christ and Antichrist: Reading Jacob 7

mi.byu.edu/pmts

A Preparatory Redemption

Reading Alma 12–13

Edited by
Matthew Bowman
Rosemary Demos

Brigham Young University
Provo, Utah

A Proceedings of the Mormon Theology Seminar book

Neal A. Maxwell Institute, Provo 84602 | maxwellinstitute.byu.edu

Library of Congress Cataloging-in-Publication Data

Names: Mormon Theology Seminar (2016 : Berkeley, Calif.), author. | Bowman, Matthew, editor. | Demos, Rosemary, editor. | Mormon Theology Seminar. Proceedings of the Mormon Theology Seminar.
Title: A preparatory redemption : reading Alma 12-13 / edited by Matthew Bowman, Rosemary Demos.
Description: Provo, Utah : Neal A. Maxwell Institute, Brigham Young University, [2018] | Series: Proceedings of the Mormon Theology Seminar | Includes bibliographical references.
Identifiers: LCCN 2018004461 | ISBN 9780842530255 (pbk. : alk. Paper)
Subjects: LCSH: Book of Mormon. Alma--Congresses. | Church of Jesus Christ of Latter-day Saints--Doctrines--Congresses. | Mormon Church--Doctrines--Congresses.
Classification: LCC BX8627 .M67 2016 | DDC 289.3/22--dc23
LC record available at https://lccn.loc.gov/2018004461

♾ This paper meets the requirements of ANSI/NISO Z39.48-1992 (Permanence of Paper).

ISBN: 978-0-8425-3025-5

Cover and book design: Jenny Webb and Andrew Heiss

Printed in the United States of America

Contents

Introduction

IN ALMA 12 AND 13, Alma the Younger and his companion, the convert Amulek, engage in dialogue with leaders of the city of Ammonihah, particularly the "lawyer" Zeezrom and the "chief ruler" Antionah (Alma 10:31–32; 12:20).[1] Like the inhabitants of their city, these men are said to be "lying and deceiving"—not only are they corrupt but they are also aware of their corruption (Alma 12:1). The city is in a state of both religious and social decay; indeed, for our redactor, Mormon, these forces are intertwined, and each reinforces the other. The people of Ammonihah are in social disorder because they are in theological disorder; they do not understand God's message, so they do not know how to run their society. At the same time, they lack proper understanding of religious doctrine because they lack proper authority by which to explain it. The discourse Alma delivers in Alma 12:19–13:20, then, should be understood as a specific response to the specific problem of Ammonihah.

That notion is all the more important to grasp because Alma's sermon is often taken in abstraction as a universal discourse on priesthood applicable in all times and all places. But rather, as these papers

1. Throughout this volume, we have used Royal Skousen, ed., *The Book of Mormon: The Earliest Text* (New Haven: Yale University Press, 2009), for our base text.

illustrate, Alma's discourse focuses essentially upon the practical question of order. He is inspired by what he takes to be Antionah's misunderstanding of the story of Adam and Eve, recorded in Alma 12:19–21, and he spins from that story broader lessons about the nature of reality itself. On the face of it, Alma's sermon moves from Adam and Eve's expulsion from the garden to a discussion of priesthood. In its fullest measure, though, his sermon is a description of the ways in which the order God has built into reality is made manifest, in ways particularly relevant to the society with which Alma is confronted.

In June 2016, because of the hard work of Robert Rees and the generosity of the Graduate Theological Union in Berkeley, California, the Mormon Theology Seminar gathered in Berkeley to consider these questions. With the generous support of the Maxwell Institute for Religious Studies at Brigham Young University, the Wheatley Institute, and the Laura F. Willes Center for Book of Mormon Studies, members of the seminar spent two weeks considering these verses and producing essays exploring these ideas. These papers approach the question of the establishment of God's order in two primary ways: in the structure of his communication with humanity, which Alma presents as following a discrete pattern, and in his organization of human society, built around the establishment of priesthood. These papers should be read as theological and speculative, rather than as definitive. The aim of the seminar is to develop through interdisciplinary collaboration a creative conversation surrounding the text, exploring its possibilities and demonstrating that the work of reading the Book of Mormon is never quite finished.

First, the question of communication. Several times in his conversations with Zeezrom and Amulek, Alma and our redactor, Mormon, make clear that communication between God and humanity must be done in order. Alma's opponents are repeatedly characterized as false and untrustworthy communicators. Alma chastises Zeezrom for his "lyings and craftiness," linking his deception to both sinfulness and the corrupt social order in Ammonihah (Alma 12:3). Zeezrom's lies were "a snare of the adversary," derived from Satan. More, Alma describes the fruits of false speech in metaphors of physical slavery and imprisonment; Satan seeks to "encircle you about with his chains," to wield the "power of his captivity," and, more immediately, to incite social unrest in Ammonihah, inciting the people to "revile us and to cast us out" (Alma 12:6, 4). Again, theological failure, political failure, and moral failure went hand in hand.

Compounding this satanic deception was the fact that the people of Ammonihah aggressively asserted that their deceptions were in fact true religion, reversing the divine order of God. Matthew Bowman's paper, "The Profession of Nehor and the Holy Order of God: Theology and Society in Ammonihah," explores the Nephite dissenting movement that appears to have had its apex in the person of Nehor and argues that by the time Alma reached the city this movement had come to dominate Ammonihah. While this movement has often been interpreted as insincere, Bowman argues that it rather promoted a sort of "meritocratic aristocracy" that celebrated success in this world over the promise of redemption in the next and that also claimed its beliefs held fidelity to scripture (Alma 1:2). In Ammonihah, for instance, Antionah claims that "the scripture" that describes God's posting of an angel with a flaming sword on guard at the way to Eden demonstrates that Alma's belief in eternal life is faulty (Alma 12:21).

Of course, Alma and Amulek reject Antionah's interpretation of scripture as faulty. For Alma, Antionah's beliefs are incorrect, not merely because they seem to him self-evidently contradicting scripture, but because, in the previous verses, he has laid out a model system of divine communication. David Gore and Rosemary Demos each explore the nature of this communication. Gore observes that Alma frequently uses the word *converse* to describe God's interactions with humanity that began at the Garden of Eden. "Every message contains informational as well as relational content," Gore argues, maintaining that Alma understood the divine communication of the sort Antionah invokes as more than factual. Reflecting, perhaps, on his own revelatory experiences, Alma believed that the contact with God he outlined invites humanity into increasingly intimate—but also covenantal—relationships that foster righteousness and ultimately salvation. Thus, Antionah's belief that the garden must always remain inaccessible seemed to Alma incomprehensible.

Demos, similarly, emphasizes the pattern of communication Alma lays out in Alma 12:28–30. First, angels appear to humanity and "caused men to behold of his glory" (Alma 12:29). Only following this encounter did God converse with human beings, endowing them with knowledge (of "the plan of redemption") and expectations ("according to their faith and repentance and their holy works") (Alma 12:29–30). For Demos, Alma here is engaging in a vast project of intertextuality, weaving together his own story with that of the exodus and of Adam and Eve to emphasize that God's miraculous, gracious power and presence precede instruction in information. However, as Demos explains, these stories also illustrate that "the grace of angelic glory is not tender or soothing, but disruptive, even violent." By "angels" Alma may well mean any commissioned messenger of God, and he could perceive his own disruptive presence in Ammonihah as representative of the order of divine communication.

The disruptive power of God's communication is itself the topic of other essays. As Gore develops his reflections from Alma's repeated use of the word *converse*, Robert Rees's reflections on Alma's use of the word *heart* extend Demos's argument. Contrasting the "hardened" heart of Alma 12:33–35, 37, with the "mighty change" of heart Alma speaks of in Alma 5:14, Rees reflects on the sometimes painful process of softening a hardened heart, arguing that it demands remembering of personal and national story, a life of holiness, and the acceptance of humility. For Rees, Alma is pleading with the Ammonihahites to build a project of remembering with him; one which might well inflict pain of the heart, but which will ultimately be worth it.

Similarly, Sheila Taylor reflects upon the precise nature of the "plan of redemption" Alma describes as part and parcel of God's communication with humanity (Alma 12:29–30). Like Rees, she reflects on the problem of hard-heartedness, concluding that "God reaches out to us. What is required of us is to be responsive." For Taylor, as for Demos, the order of God's communication is significant. As she sees it, God first reaches out to humanity, and God's response is then dictated by humanity's response. Taylor intimates that hardening hearts is in some ways natural: human pride and anxiety both lead us to that "passive" response—something we might do without thinking about it.

Repentance, then, is in some ways unnatural but is also, as with Rees, the far more fruitful path.

In the early verses of chapter 13, Alma transitions from his exhortation to the Ammonihahites to not harden their hearts to a discussion of priesthood with this curious phrasing: "I would cite your minds forward to the time when the Lord God gave these commandments unto his children. And I would that ye should remember that the Lord God ordained priests after his holy order, which was after the order of his Son, to teach these things unto the people" (Alma 13:1). Clearly, Alma seeks a link between priests, who are those "after his holy order," and the system of communication he has just finished describing. That link is embedded in the uncommon phrase "cite your minds forward." What Alma means by that phrase and what he envisions the "holy order" to be are the topic of the remaining essays.

Both Joseph Spencer and Adam Miller reflect in some way on what it might mean to cite one's mind forward. Spencer offers an extensive reading of Alma 12:31, particularly grappling with what might be called a problem of punctuation. The verse runs: "Wherefore, he gave commandments unto men, they having first transgressed the first commandments as to things which were temporal and becoming as Gods, knowing good from evil, placing themselves in a state to act, or being placed in a state to act according to their wills and pleasures, whether to do evil or to do good." Spencer asks what sort of meaning that *or* is intended to communicate and concludes that it captures an odd atemporality in the human condition. Sometimes, Spencer says, we are in a state to act knowing good from evil, sure we understand the moral parameters of our choices—but even then, Spencer notes, we often fall short of our own consciences. Other times we may act according to our wills and pleasures, feeling competent but rarely raising our gaze above the horizons of our own desires. We are then fragmented, "pretending that the void that traumatically divides us from ourselves is really just a feature of our own brilliant strategizing about how to do things in the best way possible." For Spencer, our sense of temporality, of cause and effect, is a function of our minds attempting to make sense of how little we actually understand our own motivations. Rather, Alma is calling us to perceive that God's intentions are not chronologically bound but rather exist "from the foundation of the world" (Alma 12:30; 13:3).

Alternatively, for Miller, casting one's mind forward is the ground of what Mormons call "agency." As he puts it, "Agency is grounded in this perpetual looking forward, this endless hoping and planning, this burning itch to go somewhere and to do something." When Alma instructs the people of Ammonihah that this life is "a probationary state, a time to prepare to meet God," and even "a preparatory state," this is what he means (Alma 12:24, 26). In this life, we are ceaselessly casting our minds forward, planning, preparing, in an endless state of near consummation. Instead, Miller proposes that Alma wants his listeners to focus on a certain aspect of his lesson: that the plan of salvation and the holy order each were prepared "from the foundation of the world." It is the job of the holy order, Miller posits, to remind the people of that plan of salvation through ordinances. As Alma 13:16 puts it, "Now these ordinances were given after this manner, that thereby the people might look forward on the Son of God, it being a type of his order or it being his order." Again, looking forward, this time "on the Son of God." For Miller, the ordinances the priesthood administers are reminders, not of the chronological difference between redemption and the present, but their chronological simultaneity. "From the foundation of the world" means an atemporal eternity. We are to draw our eyes away from the future and pay attention to the present, and the holy order are those whose task it is to teach us how.

The final paper, offered by Bridget Jack Jeffries, suitably concludes the collection, speculating in practical terms what that holy order might look like. Jeffries suggests that—given the demands of Ammonihah's failures—the holy order might be best understood not simply as a priestly class but as a social revision, an alternative sort of sociality modeling for the corrupt city of how God's world should stand. She argues that the primary function of priests as Alma appears to envision them is "more evangelistic than sacerdotal." Alma's priests, she maintains, are teachers chosen because of their commitment to good works and high character, and thus they serve as both models and instructors for the population at large. Indeed, Jeffries suggests, drawing a comparison between Alma's priesthood and the Protestant notion of the priesthood of all believers, Alma is concerned with ensuring that there should be no inequity between priests and nonpriests because it is important that, at least theoretically, the opportunity for priestly duties of instruction and counsel should be open to all who meet its expectations.

At the end of his discourse, Alma declares "Behold, the scriptures are before you; if ye will wrest them, it shall be to your own destruction" (Alma 13:20). Alma's confidence that scripture self-evidently challenges the claims of his interlocutors is belied by the length and detail of his address to them. Though rooted, surely, in engagement with the Hebrew scriptures, Alma's task has been far more than simply explicating them. Rather, he has confronted a society steeped in anxiety and pride and sought ways to explain to them what he understands the gifts of God to be. Alma invites his listeners to depart their world and enjoy the "rest of the Lord"; these papers explore simultaneously how meaningful and challenging that task may be (Alma 12:36).

—Matthew Bowman

Summary Report

Question 1: What are the social, political, and ideological contexts that shape Alma's sermon to the people of Ammonihah in Alma 12:19–13:20?

The people of Ammonihah are inheritors of what might be called the Nephite dissenting movement, which splintered from the church established by Alma the Elder during the reign of King Mosiah. According to Mormon, this dissenting movement was widespread; indeed, Alma the Younger himself took part in it for a time.

What is the nature of this dissenting movement? Mormon said that "because of their unbelief they could not understand the word of God" (Mosiah 26:3). This appears to mean that they did not interpret scripture in the same way those in the church did. He presents their beliefs entirely in terms of rejecting the church's orthodoxy. "They did not believe what had been said concerning the resurrection of the dead, neither did they believe concerning the coming of Christ," he wrote (Mosiah 26:2). However, other passages in Alma offer more detail. Contra Mormon's claim about the dissenters, Nehor, the greatest exponent of dissent, claimed fidelity to "the word of God" (Alma 1:3). He also taught that "all mankind should be saved at the last day and that they need not fear nor tremble, but that they might lift up their heads and rejoice, for the Lord had created all men and had also redeemed all men; and in the end all men should have eternal life" (Alma 1:4). The Amalekites, who appear later in the Book of Mormon and declare that they are "after the order of the Nehors," rejected similar ideas: "the coming of Christ and . . . the resurrection of the dead and that there could be no redemption for mankind save it were through the death and sufferings of Christ" (Alma 21:4, 9). Rejection of the notion of sin and therefore the need for an atonement of Christ appears to be universal among various streams of the Nephite dissenting movement, though their beliefs about the afterlife and resurrection seem a bit tougher to pin down. Zeezrom seems ignorant of the resurrection in Alma 12:8, and Antionah appears to deny it a few verses later. This is difficult to reconcile with Nehor's insistence that all men should have eternal life. It is probably more useful to think of Nehorism as one strand of a broader dissenting movement that evolved across both time and space.

The dissenting movement seems to have inspired a series of rules about religion. The transition from Mosiah's kingship to the reign of the judges followed the establishment of Alma's church and paralleled the rise of the Nephite dissenting movement. These tumultuous events were accompanied with a series of decrees about religion. Mosiah declared "there should not any unbeliever persecute any of those which belonged to the church of God" (Mosiah 27:2). Likewise, within the church "there was a strict command throughout all the churches that there should be no persecutions among them" (v. 3). More, "priests and teachers should labor with their own hands for their support" (v. 5). After he describes Nehor's rise and fall, which occurs soon after these decrees, Alma summarizes the state of affairs: "the law could have no power on any man for their belief" (Alma 1:17).

The very existence of these decrees demonstrates that religion was causing political and social tension in Nephite society. Ammonihah is a useful case study. Nehor sought to upset the careful social and cultural balance Mosiah and Alma had implemented. He demanded "that every priest and teacher had ought to become popular and they ought not to labor with their own hands, but that they had ought to be supported by the people" (Alma 1:3). In this same vein, Alma claims Nehor sought "riches and honor" (Alma 1:16). And given that in Alma 2 the Nehorite Amlici sought to reestablish a monarchy, we might see Nehorism as an attempt to renew Nephite aristocracy.

Alma's confrontation with the people of Ammonihah in Alma 12–13 should therefore be understood against the backdrop of these religious and political tensions. In Alma 14:5, the people testified that Alma and Amulek "had reviled against the law and their lawyers and the judges of the land and also all the people that were in the land, and also testified that there was but one God and that he should send his Son among the people, but he should not save them." Note the links here between the violation of the law and the contradiction of theology. The people of Ammonihah understood these two things to be one and the same. When Alma and Amulek enter the city, they are confronted by lawyers, like Zeezrom, and chief rulers, like Antionah, who challenge Alma on the grounds that while he was once chief judge, he is no more, and that their church has no claim upon them. More, the accusations against Alma and Amulek echo earlier Nephite rules against religious persecution.

In Alma 12–13, Alma emphasizes a few themes that illustrate this question of the conflation of religious and political authority. First, he states that their interpretation of scripture is faulty because they lack authoritative interpreters. His invocation of Genesis, Exodus, Psalms, and Hebrews culminates in his frustrated declaration to the people of Ammonihah that they have the scriptures before them and that it is their fault if they interpret them incorrectly: "Behold, the scriptures are before you; if ye will wrest them, it shall be to your own destruction" (Alma 13:20). Second, Alma spends a great deal of time exploring the notion of priesthood, attempting to explain to the people of Ammonihah that though they perceive his authority to be faulty and illegal, it is in fact derived from God and hence has inherent legitimacy. His frequent repetition of the word *remember* is striking: Alma believes these people once recognized correct authority, but have since forgotten it. In invoking scripture and priestly authority, then, Alma is attempting to correct the particular errors he sees in Ammonihah.

Question 2: What role does scripture play in shaping Alma's sermon to the people of Ammonihah in Alma 12:19–13:20? What scriptural texts are central to the debate?

It is not clear what role physical texts (e.g., on plates or scrolls) play in framing the events of Alma 12–13. It is uncertain whether Alma and his interlocutors are literally reading passages and referring to texts open before them or simply reciting or "rehearsing" key passages from memory. It is clear, however, that Alma and the people of Ammonihah share a scriptural tradition, and allusions to both the language and narrative of this tradition are abundant throughout these chapters. In this regard, Alma 12–13 is deeply intertextual and echoes both biblical and Book of Mormon sources.

As Alma takes it upon himself to "unfold the scriptures" to the people of Ammonihah, the authority of these scriptures to dictate divine truth is a consistent question (Alma 12:1). Alma's intertextual allusions demonstrate the assumption that his own personal authority, as well as the validity of his doctrine, can be defended or debunked with scriptural texts. However, his consistent plea that the people search the scriptures rather than "wresting" or distorting them demonstrates the ambiguity of scriptural interpretation as well (see Alma 13:20). This narrative raises questions about the relationship between texts and truths: Why do Alma and the people of Ammonihah come to such conflicting interpretations of sacred texts? Do the people of Ammonihah deliberately reject the truth claims of scripture? Or do they value scripture but reject Alma's particular interpretative stance?

The section of text under consideration here opens with a challenge to Alma's understanding of a specific citation from Genesis. The controversy of scriptural interpretation is established as Antionah calls upon Alma to justify a seeming contradiction between belief and text. This text becomes the premise for subsequent theological debate: both Alma and Antionah reflect on the Genesis narrative of the expulsion from Eden in order to extract from it truths regarding the nature and purpose of death and the resurrection.

But Alma's expansive response to Antionah's challenge goes far beyond the initial close reading of this single reference. Alma continues with implicit references to the exodus narrative, references that can be identified by tracing specific choices of diction. For example, the "provocations" described in Alma 12:36 echo the language of Hebrews 3, Psalm 95, and Jacob 1. Each of these chapters uses "provocation" to invoke the exodus narrative and describe the wayward behavior of the Israelites of Moses's day. Alma continues with an explication of the pre-Israelite history of Melchizedek and Abraham. While Alma 13 echoes descriptions of Melchizedek's role found in Psalm 110, Hebrews 7, and Genesis 14, Alma's own characterization of Melchizedek adds details not drawn specifically from these known sources but supportive of Alma's own theological discourse. In addition to these biblical references, Alma also weaves into his sermon threads of his own conversion story. While it is unclear whether the people of Ammonihah would recognize this personal narrative as a sacred text in its own right, Alma constructs his conversion experience as a story of spiritual deliverance that parallels the covenant narrative of the Israelite nation.

Thus, while Alma freely expounds in his own voice on topics such as priesthood, typology, mankind's agency, and the role of angels, the intertextuality of his discourse also frames these topics with an appeal to the authority of scriptural tradition. The ultimate rejection of this authority is demonstrated in the city's public burning of the very texts out of which Alma preaches (cf. Alma 14:8). The challenge to scriptural authority introduced earlier in the reading is thus twofold. First is the challenge to personal authority, as the people of Ammonihah question Alma and Amulek's claims to religious leadership. But also implicit in this story is a challenge to the authority of the scriptural tradition itself. In Ammonihah, both the message and messengers of sacred text have the potential to become social and doctrinal threats.

Question 3: In Alma 13:3, Alma describes an order of priests who were "called and prepared from the foundation of the world." In the context of Alma's

discourse, what does it mean to be called and prepared from the foundation of the world? Is this a reference to the doctrine of premortal life?

In Alma 13:3, Alma describes an order of priests "called and prepared from the foundation of the world." Though this formula has sometimes been taken to hint at a doctrine of human premortal life in the Book of Mormon, this does not appear to be the most likely reading.

Twice in relation to being called and prepared from the foundation of the world, Alma also uses the phrase "in the first place." Alma 13:3 claims that these priests, "in the first place," were "left to choose good or evil, therefore they having chosen good and exercising exceeding great faith are called with a holy calling." Alma emphasizes this same connection between goodness, faith, and a holy calling in verse 5 when he notes that "in the first place," those who did not receive this ordination "were on the same standing with their brethren."

However, several factors mitigate against the likelihood of this "first place" referring to a premortal existence. First, and perhaps most importantly, the doctrine of human premortal life as commonly understood in contemporary Mormonism is, apart from this potential instance, tellingly and consistently absent from the Book of Mormon's own account of the plan of redemption. Second, Alma explicitly frames the business of "being called and prepared from the foundation of the world" as something that has happened "according to the foreknowledge of God" (Alma 13:3). That is, Alma himself expressly accounts for the anticipatory character of this holy calling in terms of God's foreknowledge, rather than in terms of human premortal existence. Third, earlier in this same sermon, Alma repeatedly uses the language of "first" to refer to our "first parents" in Eden (Alma 12:21, 26), to the "first commandments" given to them there (v. 31), and to the "first provocation" of God's wrath that resulted from their transgression of those commandments (v. 36). That is, if the "first place" refers to a particular place, then Alma's sermon has primed us to read that first place as a reference to Eden. However, given the complexity of mapping Alma's comments about the holy order onto his earlier discussion of Eden, the simplest (and blandest) available reading of "in the first place" may, in this instance, be likely. That is, rather than indicating a prior time or place that preceded mortality, the phrase may just indicate logical priority. The phrase "in the first place . . ." would then simply amount to a mild way of saying "the first reason is that . . ." Regardless, on any reading, the phrase appears problematic. And, ultimately, the phrase certainly appears too problematic to justify, by itself, a doctrine of premortal life.

In counterpoint to the uncertainty that problematizes his use of the phrase "in the first place," Alma precisely and consistently employs the more crucial formula, "from the foundation of the world," in a way that does not invoke human premortality. Alma uses the formula five times in this section of his sermon. In Alma 12:25 it refers to "the plan of redemption which was laid from the foundation of the world," and in Alma 12:30 to "the plan of redemption which had been prepared from the foundation of the world" (Alma 12:25 and 33 also use truncated versions of this same formula, referring to "a plan of redemption laid").

Strikingly, in Alma 12:32, Alma distinguishes this primordial plan of redemption from the commandments that God would later, and in stages, make known: "God gave unto them commandments *after* having made known unto them the plan of redemption." Where the plan of redemption is laid from the foundation of the world, the commandments are given "after" the plan of redemption has already been made known. The plan of redemption, by Alma's account, is not God's post hoc response to human wickedness and frailty. More, it is worth noting that, apparently, God can make the plan of redemption known *without* having first given commandments to the children of men. This inversion is curious: the solution (redemption) seems, according to Alma's account, to definitively displace and precede the problem (the transgression of commandments).

Though Alma does not associate God's commandments with "the foundation of the world," he does use the formula three additional times in Alma 13, all in connection with what he calls the "holy order of God" (Alma 13:6). This parallel alignment of both the plan of redemption and the holy order with the foundation of the world establishes a decisive connection between the two. The plan of redemption is, in some crucial way, synonymous with the holy order of God. In Alma

13:3, priests of this order are "called and prepared from the foundation of the world." In verse 5, the "holy calling" (rather than the priests themselves) is described as "being prepared from the foundation of the world." And in verse 7, coupled with some instructive elaboration, the order itself, "this high priesthood . . . after the order of his Son," is said to be "from the foundation of the world, or in other words, being without beginning of days or end of years, being prepared from eternity to all eternity according to his foreknowledge of all things."

With this gloss on what is meant by the foundation of the world ("from the foundation of the world, or in other words . . ."), Alma 13:7 offers an especially significant example of the sermon's more or less continuous appropriation and transformation of a constellation of formulas native to the book of Hebrews. This language clusters around the figure of Melchizedek (see Alma 13:14–19) but tracks across the whole of Hebrews 3, 4, and 7. In this instance, the proximate parallel for the language about "the foundation of the world" is Hebrews 4:3: "For we which have believed do enter into rest, as he said, As I have sworn in my wrath, if they shall enter into my rest: although the works were finished from the foundation of the world." Here, "God's works" are described as having been finished from the foundation of the world. The works in question are the work of creating or "founding" the world itself. Upon completing the work of founding the world, God then "rested" on the seventh day. This already completed work is the issue, both for the author of Hebrews and for Alma: both are concerned with what it means to finish one's work and "enter into the rest of God" (Alma 12:37; cf. Alma 12:34, 35, 36; 13:6, 12, 13, 16), and this rest is exemplified by the Sabbath into which God enters following the work of creation.

Alma, though, in the process of adapting this language, appears to fundamentally change the formula. In 13:7, he conjoins this passage in Hebrews 4:3 with language proper to Hebrews 7:3, a verse that describes Melchizedek as being "without father, without mother, without descent, having neither beginning of days, nor end of life; but made like unto the Son of God; abideth a priest continually." Here, Alma disjoins this enigmatic description from the person of Melchizedek, appends it to the holy order itself, and then rereads the "foundation of the world" as meaning something that is itself "without beginning of days or end of years." Where Hebrews 4:3 uses "foundation of the world" to refer to the enumerated days of God's work of creating or founding the world, Alma instead appropriates and then glosses this formula to refer to something that defies mortal chronology and has no beginning of days or end of years. Where Hebrews reads "foundation of the world" as a reference to God's past tense and completed act of creation, Alma takes up this language of creating the world, declares this foundation to be the holy order after the Son of God, and then reads this holy order as being always already "prepared from eternity to all eternity" (Alma 13:7).

This transformation resonates with the other set of key terms to which Alma repeatedly returns in his attempt to unfold the connection between the plan of redemption and the holy order of God. As Alma explains it, the holy order is crucial to the plan of redemption because the ordinances proper to that order are "given after this manner, that thereby the people might look forward on the Son of God, it being a type of his order or it being his order—and this that they might look forward to him for a remission of their sins, that they might enter into the rest of the Lord" (Alma 13:16). Or, as he puts it in 13:2, "those priests were ordained after the order of his Son in a manner that thereby the people might know in what manner to look forward to his Son for redemption." Alma insists that the holy order is crucial to God's plan of redemption because it exemplifies a certain "manner" of looking forward to the Son for redemption. In the end, the entire sermon turns on an elaboration of this "manner" of looking forward.

In 13:16, Alma describes this messianic manner of looking as typological ("it being a type of his order"). Rather than relating to redemption chronologically as a distant future event, the people are urged to relate to their redemption typologically as already prepared and accomplished from the foundation of the world. A tightly parallel passage in Jarom 1:11 confirms and clarifies this point. There, we're told that "the prophets and the priests and the teachers did labor diligently, exhorting with all long-suffering the people to diligence, . . . persuading them to look forward unto the Messiah and believe in him to come as though he already was. And after this manner did they teach them." Here we have all of Alma's key terms: *priests*, *manner*, and *looking forward*. However, instead of using the word *type*, Jarom 1:11 simply gives a description of what it means to look at something typologically: to look forward to the Son in a manner that is typological is to "believe in him to come as though he already was."

Throughout this sermon, Alma uses language that defies chronology and privileges typology. The plan of redemption and the rest of the Lord, treated typologically, are understood to be already available from the foundation of the world. The plan of redemption, as we've seen, is laid from the foundation of the world and, thus, surprisingly antedates both God's commandments and any transgression of those commandments. In this same way, the holy order of God is pivotal to entering into the rest of the Lord because it displays in exemplary fashion this "manner" of looking forward that, like God's foreknowledge, sees the future as already given in the past. Though the contemporary Mormon doctrine of human premortal life is partially mirrored in this typological gesture of seeing the future in the past, the whole of Alma's sermon is best understood in terms of typology itself.

Question 4: In Alma 12:19–13:20, how does God "make known" his purposes to human beings? What are the divine means of communication?

Before Alma says anything in his response to Antionah about priests and priesthood in Alma 13:1–20, he addresses at least two other ways that God seeks to communicate with human beings in Alma 12:19–37. Understanding these additional lines of communication, along with their stated motivations, should help clarify how Alma understands the specific role played by priests.

The question of communication between God and human beings arises, according to Alma, because of an expedience. "And after God had appointed that these things"—"these things" meaning, at the very least, death and judgment (see Alma 12:27)—"should come unto man, behold, then he saw that it was expedient that man should know concerning the things whereof he had appointed unto them" (Alma 12:28). Although the word *expedient* is often assumed by readers of the Book of Mormon to mean simply "necessary" or "important," its literal meaning concerns urgency and haste—as in the verb *to expedite.* Alma's claim, then, suggests that the circumstances attending human beings, once they had been removed from their Edenic paradise, were urgent. God felt some urgency to communicate with human beings about their situation, especially about their ultimate appointment with death and judgment (see, again, Alma 12:27).

According to Alma's account, communication between God and human beings unfolds in several stages. In response to the recognized expedience, God first "sent angels to converse with [human beings], which caused men to behold of his glory" (Alma 12:29). This first encounter resulted in a redirection of human attention to God: "they began from that time forth to call on his name" (v. 30). In response to such prayer, next "God conversed with men," ultimately communicating two distinct things. First, he "made known unto them the plan of redemption" (v. 30). And second, "he gave commandments unto men," spiritual commandments to replace the transgressed temporal commandments given in Eden (v. 31).

There are, then, three discernible moments in this initial sequence of communications: (1) an angelic encounter; (2) a consequent human petition to God; (3) a culminating communication from God himself.

Alma gives far more of his discourse to clarifying the third of these three moments, but there is much significance in the first two as well. Latter-day Saints will not be surprised by the idea that God sends angels to prepare the way for human beings to converse with him directly and personally. Nor will they be surprised by the idea that the primary result of the angels' intervention is a redirection of human beings to God in petition: "They began from that time forth to call on his name" (Alma 12:30). But the details of Alma's description of these two sequences are suggestive.

It should be noted that the angels (perhaps equivalent with the cherubim placed to guard the way to the tree of life?) are sent specifically "to converse with" human beings, but that what they actually accomplish seems to be nonconversational; they "caused men to behold of [God's] glory" (Alma 12:29). These words could, of course, be read in a variety of ways, but one distinct possibility is that, although angels *are* sent to communicate with human beings, the shock of their appearance often frustrates any such purpose—with the result that they tend instead just to cause their would-be interlocutors to "behold of [God's] glory" (v. 29). Certainly, Alma himself experienced such a thing. In his encounter with an angel, he missed most of the angel's message due to the shock of the experience. In his own words: "And the angel spake more things unto me, which were heard by my brethren, but I did not hear them. For when I heard the words, if thou wilt be destroyed of thyself, seek no more to destroy the church of God, I was struck with such great fear and amazement lest perhaps I should be destroyed that I fell to the earth and I did hear no more" (Alma 36:11). Here the angel represents a kind of *failure* to communicate or to converse, but with the crucial result that Alma gives himself (after a period of resistance) to the task of calling on the Lord's name: "I cried within my heart: O Jesus, thou Son of God, have mercy on me" (v. 18). Whatever actually takes place in the course of an angelic encounter, Alma seems ultimately interested in how such experiences pave the way for direct conversation between God and human beings.

Although Alma presents angelic encounters in terms of the shock of the transcendent, he presents the encounter between human beings and God himself in strikingly mundane terms. "God conversed with men and made known unto them the plan of redemption," and then "he gave commandments unto men" (Alma 12:30–31). Where encounters with angels are a matter of shock and glory, encounters with God are a question of communication. That is, they are at least in part a question of an actual transfer of information, although the verb *to converse* suggests more than just the transfer of information. Given the nineteenth-century resonance of the verb *to converse* ("to keep company; to associate; to cohabit; to hold intercourse and be intimately acquainted," according to the 1828 first edition of Webster's *Dictionary*), intimacy and communion are also characteristic of God's successful conversation with human beings—an intimacy and a communion that are arguably lacking in angelic encounter. But whether informative revelation or divine self-disclosure is to be emphasized in connection with encounters with God, their relative banality when compared with the visit of angels in Alma's discourse is arresting.

As already noted, according to Alma, God communicates two distinct things in the course of his conversation with human beings. First, he makes known "the plan of redemption" (Alma 12:30). Second, he provides a set of "commandments" (v. 31). Although each of these is discussed at first in relatively short order, Alma comes back to each of them in the course of his discussion, providing much more detail. He dedicates three verses (see vv. 33–35) to a full articulation of God's communication of the plan of redemption, presented as a direct quotation of God's actual words. And then he dedicates no fewer than nine verses (see Alma 13:1–9) to a lengthy description of the occasion on which God first "gave these commandments unto his children" (v. 1).

As regards the first of these two communications, Alma describes God as "call[ing] on men in the name of his Son" in communicating "the plan of redemption" directly (Alma 12:33)—this in clear parallel to human beings' own "call[ing] on his name" in petition (v. 30). This match of call for call, of summons for summons, suggests mutual interest and attachment. And importantly, God's outline of the plan of redemption as Alma quotes it concerns first and foremost questions of the heart. Three times in three verses, God mentions the importance of not hardening one's heart, twice he refers to mercy, and once—less comfortingly—he refers to wrath. The plan of redemption is a matter of the heart, and the first full knowing of God thus seems to be a knowing of the heart (something Alma emphasizes when he then exhorts his hearers to have soft hearts themselves; see vv. 36–37).

As Alma turns his attention from the first to the second of God's conversational topics, he shifts his attention from hearts to minds: "I would cite your minds forward to the time which the Lord God gave these commandments unto his children" (Alma 13:1). The commandments, it seems, concern more the knowing of the mind than the knowing of the heart. Moreover, and crucially, Alma explains that God communicates his commandments to most human beings through mediators rather than directly. To make his commandments known to his children, "the Lord God ordained priests . . . to teach these things unto the people" (v. 1). The commandments, it seems, were given quite directly just to some, to persons granted "great privilege" because they did not "reject the Spirit of God on account of the hardness of their hearts" (v. 4). With hearts in the right place, some at least are prepared to have their minds focused on spiritual things. But then these priests have the responsibility to assist others to "look forward to [God's] Son for redemption" (v. 2). All minds end up directed to the heart-based plan of redemption, whether in direct conversation with God or thanks to the work of priests and especially the "manner" of their ordination (vv. 2, 7, 16).

Question 5: In Alma 12:19–37, what is the relationship between what Alma calls being "in a state to act" and his closely related descriptions of "temporal death" and "judgment"? Or, in short, what does agency have to do with death and judgment?

In Alma 12:20–21, Antionah attempts to rebut the message that Alma and Amulek have delivered to Zeezrom and the people of Ammonihah. In particular, he objects to Alma's claims about a resurrection. Citing the biblical account of the fall, Antionah assumes that death is the end and that God never intended people to live forever. He asks: "What does this scripture mean which saith that God placed cherubims and a flaming sword on the east of the garden of Eden lest our first parents should enter and partake of the fruit of the tree of life and live forever? And thus we see that there was no possible chance that they should live forever" (Alma 12:21). Essentially, Antionah asks Alma: How is resurrection possible if God himself has, from the time of the fall, intentionally blocked the way to the tree of life?

In response, Alma admits that, because Adam and Eve had partaken of the fruit of the tree of knowledge of good and evil, "all mankind became a lost and a fallen people" (Alma 12:22). But Alma takes this phrase, "a lost and a fallen people," to refer to mankind's *dual* appointments with death and judgment. That is, he thinks humanity's lost and fallen condition involves both a "temporal death" and a "second death" (vv. 24, 32). This first death, temporal death, comes after the fall because access to the tree of life has been barred. Without access to the tree of life, physical death is inescapable. This first death is an "end" in the sense that it brings mortality to a close. However, Alma also argues that temporal death is not the ultimate end. The plan of redemption brings about the resurrection of the dead, which means that temporal death is temporary. For Alma, judgment—not death—is the real end. Judgment, though, raises the specter of a second kind of death, one that is spiritual rather than temporal. And, unlike mortality, this postjudgment state is said to be endless.

What is the nature of this endless state? It has two valences: (1) it may be a postjudgment life with God, or (2) it may be a postjudgment life without God. Alma contrasts these two states in terms of the difference between entering the "rest" of God and suffering the "wrath" of God (cf. Alma 12:37). Because the wrath of God is also described as the "everlasting destruction" of the soul, this second, spiritual death can also be seen as an end (v. 36). However, like temporal death, it can also be overcome by the plan of redemption. But in this second case, redemption is contingent on one's choices—specifically, the choice to repent and not harden one's heart.

From the substance of his attempted rebuttal, it appears that Antionah has no conception of this second appointment or final reckoning. He is ignorant of judgment. He thinks only of the first death. This smaller perspective constrains his sense of what is possible in mortality. Alma, on the other hand, wants to show Antionah and the people of Ammonihah how to redeem mortality. That is, he wants to show them how to see mortal time and temporal death as gifts that must not only be acknowledged but also received.

Death defines the length and character of human life. The imminence of death infuses life with both urgency and intensity. But if death is only a temporary end, if resurrection is promised and judgment is inevitable, then mortality, while retaining its urgency and intensity, is transformed into "a preparatory state" where repentance is possible (Alma 12:26). If Adam and Eve had immediately eaten of the fruit of the tree of life, Alma explains, there would have been no death, and they would have been "forever miserable" (v. 26). There would have been no space for repentance, no time to prepare for judgment. In this sense, temporal death—insofar as it is postponed for a time—is transformed into a gift. Adam and Eve die, but they do not immediately die upon eating the forbidden fruit. Instead of an immediate death, they are given both death *and time*—time to repent before they die. The cherubims and flaming sword have given a real gift. They have stopped human beings from confronting "that endless state . . . which is after the resurrection of the dead" before they are prepared to do so (v. 24). Possessing only a knowledge of good and evil without the additional gift of time to develop their ability to choose the good, Adam and Eve would have been consigned to an endless state of misery.

Adam and Eve arguably possess some degree of agency in the Garden of Eden. They chose to eat the forbidden fruit (cf. Alma 12:22). But it is only after the fall that their agency is fully realized. After the fall they know good and evil and are empowered, by the bounded time of their mortal lives, to "act according to their wills and pleasures, whether to do evil or to do good" (v. 31). As Alma puts it, Adam and Eve had become "as Gods, knowing good from evil, placing themselves in a state to act, or being placed in a state to act according to their wills and pleasures, whether to do evil or to do good" (v. 31). Note the curious restatement inserted into the middle of this explanation. Through their actions, Alma says, Adam and Eve had (1) actively placed *themselves* in a state to act (they had eaten the fruit), even as (2) they *were placed* in that same state (by the additional mercy of a probationary time before death).

In a similar way, Adam and Eve's new "state to act" was now structured not only by the commandment "that they should not do evil" but also by an additional call to repent (Alma 12:32). "God did call on men in the name of his Son, this being the plan of redemption which was laid, saying: If ye will repent and harden not your hearts, then will I have mercy upon you through mine Only Begotten Son" (v. 33). Here, God calls upon humans to (1) repent and (2) harden not their hearts. That is, for mercy to be efficacious, humans must both actively do something (i.e., repent) even as they passively refrain from doing something (i.e., hardening their hearts).

In this preparatory state—a state structured by death, death's delay, and the promise of a coming judgment—agency plays out between these poles of activity and restraint.

Question 6: How are priesthood and, more specifically, the "holy order" understood in Alma 13:1–20?

Alma 13 may be best known by readers of the Book of Mormon as a chapter on the priesthood, especially because it contains the Book of Mormon's only substantive statement on Melchizedek. Numerous details in the text, however, suggest that the notion of priesthood assumed by Alma in his discourse is distinct from what Latter-day Saints understand by the concept.

First, it should be noted that the "priests" described in Alma 13 have as their primary responsibility "to teach," specifically to communicate certain "commandments unto [God's] children" (Alma 13:1). There is certainly talk of rituals or ordinances in Alma 13, but it seems exclusively focused on the rituals or ordinances by which the priests in question *become* priests. That is, the only ordinances that seem to be actually mentioned in the text are, specifically, *ordinations* (see vv. 2, 3, 6, 8, 10). (It might be noted that the preceding chapter refers to "holy works" that follow or accompany "faith and repentance"—see Alma 12:30—but nothing in Alma's speech directly connects these to priesthood.) It thus appears that the sort of priesthood Alma attaches to "the holy order" has as its primary and perhaps sole responsibility to preach and to teach. This accords well with what Alma (as well as the narrator of Alma's story) says elsewhere about the holy order (see Alma 4:20; 5, chapter heading; 5:44; 6:8; 8:4; 43:2).

Second, it seems that "the holy order" represents a rather specific kind of priestly work. References to the holy order never appear in the Bible, and within the Book of Mormon they appear—with one exception (in 2 Nephi 6:2)—always in direct relationship to Alma the Younger. Evidence therefore suggests that the holy order should be understood as something largely unique to Alma's time period within the Book of Mormon, and perhaps to the still-young Nephite Christian church over which he presided as high priest. (It is possible that there was a unique precedent for Alma in Nephi's brother Jacob, the only other person to mention a "holy order" in the Book of Mormon. It may be significant, in fact, that Mormon later suggests that Alma's church revitalized a much earlier religious tradition; see 3 Nephi 5:12.)

The timing within the Book of Mormon's larger narrative for Alma's sudden cluster of references to the holy order suggests that it is meant to be contrasted with "the order of Nehor" (Alma 24:29), which takes its rise shortly after Alma becomes the head of the church and shortly before the text begins to speak of Alma's holy order.

Third, there is some textual evidence suggesting that Alma's holy order might best be understood along the lines of a monastic order. (This possibility might be strengthened by the contrast between Alma's holy order and the Nehorite order, given the latter's emphasis on priestly popularity and what the Book of Mormon calls priestcraft. By contrast, Alma's holy order seems emphatically insistent on a kind of priestly poverty; see Alma 30:31–35.) At least outside of Alma 13, the Book of Mormon speaks of the holy order occasionally as something "wherewith [people are] brought into [Alma's] church, having been sanctified by the Holy Spirit" (Alma 5:54), or as something "by" which one is "ordained" by "being baptized unto repentance and sent forth to preach among the people" (Alma 49:30). Similar in spirit, although without reference to the holy order, is Moroni 6:1, which states that "elders, priests, and teachers were baptized"—oddly as if baptism were the precise means of ordination. Alma 7:22 also seems to indicate that everyone in Gideon had been "received" into "the holy order of God." Such references can be taken together to imply that the holy order was a kind of monastic subgroup within the Nephite church rather than a hierarchically positioned group of leaders. If so, the holy order in question has less to do with administration and may have nothing to do with distinctions drawn in Latter-day Saint history between groups allowed or disallowed to hold priesthood offices.

Fourth, there is much to learn from Alma's references to Melchizedek. Although readers generally assume that these references simply indicate that Alma's "holy order" is what today goes by the name of the Melchizedek Priesthood, the context suggests that things are more complex than such a simple reference. A basic motivation for Alma's use of Melchizedek and the holy order seems to lie in the fact that his listeners in Ammonihah are not—as they themselves emphasize in response to Alma's initial preaching—members of his church, with the consequence that he has "no power over" them (Alma 8:12). Because they reject his authority as "high priest over the church" (v. 11), Alma seems to turn his attention to a kind of high priesthood that outstrips the ecclesiastical authority of the Nephite church. His listeners in Ammonihah clearly believe the book of Genesis to be inspired (see one Ammonihahite's prooftexting use of Genesis 3:24 in Alma 12:20–21), so Alma's use of the Melchizedek story from Genesis 14 seems to be motivated by his belief that, whatever the people in Ammonihah might think of the priestly authority of leaders within the Nephite Christian church, they are committed to trusting in the priestly institutions outlined in Genesis. These details suggest that Alma understands the holy order he associates with Melchizedek to be in some sense larger or more universal than the church originally organized by his father. (See, in a similar vein, Helaman 8:18.)

All of these considerations, taken together, sketch a general picture of the priesthood Alma discusses in Alma 13. Rather than something largely equivalent to the Melchizedek Priesthood or the high priesthood as this is understood in the Latter-day Saint tradition today, it seems to be something largely local within the Book of Mormon. Apparently by way of direct contrast to the Nehorite order inaugurated just a few years before the Ammonihah experience, but also as a revitalization of earlier (and perhaps largely lost) traditions associated with Nephi's brother Jacob and (much earlier) Melchizedek himself, Alma seems to have organized a priestly (and perhaps quasi-monastic) order that took as its sole responsibility to teach commandments originally given to Adam and Eve. For Alma, this priestly order was in some sense more capacious than any hierarchical priesthood associated with his church, allowing it to speak to non-Christian Nephites.

The Profession of Nehor and the Holy Order of God: Theology and Society in Ammonihah

Matthew Bowman

When Alma arrives in Ammonihah, he finds himself spurned by the population for, in essence, lacking the institutional authority they deem legitimate. "And now we know that because we are not of thy church, we know that thou hast no power over us. And thou hast delivered up the judgment seat unto Nephihah; therefore thou art not the chief judge over us," the people of Ammonihah tell him (Alma 8:12). This argument reflects the tumultuous social and political changes Alma had seen in his lifetime. By the time Alma reached Ammonihah in roughly 82 BC, Nephite society had grown increasingly diverse and its structures of authority increasingly decentralized. The book of Mosiah saw a rapid multiplication of cultural groups in the Nephite world. Similarly, ten years before Alma's visit, King Mosiah had abolished the monarchy in favor of a judgeship, elected by the voice of the people (see Mosiah 29:29). The relationship between the church and the state had grown significantly more tenuous since the time Alma the Elder had founded his church in Zarahemla. At that point, King Mosiah held ultimate authority over the church, though throughout his reign he sought to minimize the relationship between church and state. When Alma tried to persuade Mosiah to enforce orthodoxy, the king declined, and yet Alma's attempt indicates that the relationship was still relatively undefined (see Mosiah 26:10–11). Instead, by the end of his reign, Mosiah declared "there should not any unbeliever persecute any of those who belonged to the church of God" (Mosiah 27:2). Reflecting Mosiah's lead, within Alma's church there emerged a "strict command throughout all the churches that there should be no persecutions among them" (Mosiah 27:3). Moreover, "priests and teachers should labor with their own hands for their support" (Mosiah 27:5). Eventually Mormon summarizes the state of affairs: "The law could have no power on any man for their belief" (Alma 1:17).

The Nephite dissenting movement, which appears to hold power in Ammonihah when Alma arrives there, seems in part to have risen in response to these changes and in part to have caused them. This movement is easily read as simple, and even insincere, heresy.[1] As the older generation always does, Mormon blames the problem on the kids, who were "little children at the time he [King Benjamin] spake unto his people; and they did not believe the tradition of their fathers" (Mosiah 26:1). But closer attention to the dissenting movement's origins, its advocates' confrontation with Alma the Younger (himself an apostate from the movement), and the regime it seems to have established in Ammonihah reveals instead a complex network of religious belief and

1. Commenters frequently call these dissenters sophists, following Hugh Nibley's interpretation. While there is something to the comparison—dissenting leaders are frequently praised for their skill in rhetoric—I argue that they have a consistent ideology, which the label *sophist* ignores; this is why I prefer the term *Nephite dissenting movement*. Hugh Nibley, *The Ancient State: The Rulers and the Ruled* (Salt Lake City: Deseret Book and FARMS, 1991), 243–50; and *An Approach to the Book of Mormon* (Salt Lake City: Deseret Book and FARMS, 1988), 361–62, which edges uncomfortably close to stereotype. See also Douglas J. Merrell, "The False Priests of the Book of Mormon," in *Selections from the Religious Education Student Symposium, 2005* (Provo, UT: Religious Studies Center, Brigham Young University, 2005), 85–93; and Matthew Scott Stenson, "Answering for His Order: Alma's Clash with the Nehors," *BYU Studies Quarterly* 55/2 (2016): 127–53. Stenson places the people of Ammonihah in this broader sophist tradition; S. Kent Brown, "Ammonihah: Measuring Mormon's Purposes," in *A Witness for the Restoration: Essays in Honor of Robert J. Matthews*, ed. Kent P. Jackson and Andrew C. Skinner (Provo, UT: Religious Studies Center, Brigham Young University, 2007), 165–75, traces them only to Nehor.

social order far beyond Mormon's simple interpretation. The Nephite dissenting movement put forward a meritocratic aristocracy, which stood in opposition to the devolved power of the society Alma and Mosiah had created. Alma the Younger's campaign in Ammonihah, then, should be understood not simply as a theological refutation of heresy, but an invocation of a different way of understanding social organization and authority, what Alma the Younger calls the holy order. While the Nephite dissenting movement associates religious practice with economic gain and political authority, Alma urges the creation of an egalitarian society opposed to inequality and hierarchy.

The reforms of Alma and Mosiah seem predicated on a suspicion of aristocracy due to a persistent suspicion that power leads to sin and decentralization leads to righteousness. When Mosiah renounces the throne, he recalls King Noah's concern that "the sins of many people have been caused by the iniquities of their kings; therefore their iniquities are answered upon the heads of their kings" (Mosiah 29:31). Instead Mosiah insists that "it is not common that the voice of the people desireth any thing contrary to that which is right" (Mosiah 29:26). Mosiah places his faith in the many rather than in the few, believing—or hoping—that "unequality should be no more in this land, especially among this my people. But I desire that this land be a land of liberty and every man may enjoy his rights and privileges alike" (Mosiah 29:32). Contemporary Americans may read this passage as an endorsement of political democracy, but Mosiah appears to be speaking rather in moral and religious terms, arguing that a society in which moral responsibility is decentralized is the most likely to foster righteous citizens.[2] It is telling, then, that Alma's church embraces decentralization of power. Mosiah directs that "all their priests and teachers should labor with their own hands for their support" (Mosiah 27:5). Alma the Younger serves ten years as the first elected judge of the people but decides to resign in order, as Mormon puts it, "that

2. Richard Bushman's observations in "The Book of Mormon and the American Revolution," in *Believing History: Latter-day Saint Essays*, ed. Reid L. Neilson and Jed Woodworth (New York: Columbia University Press, 2004), 47–65, are relevant to this point.

he himself might go forth among his people, or among the people of Nephi, that he might preach the word of God unto them" (Alma 4:19). This was apparently not possible while he served in the judgment seat; rather, Alma becomes convinced that centralization of power prevents him from preaching successfully.

The Nephite dissenting movement appears to have objected not only to the theology of Alma's church but also to its embrace of Mosiah's philosophy of decentralization. Though the dissenting movement appears to have emerged at least a decade before his own rise to influence, the leading figure appears to have been Nehor, whose ideas were present in the dissenting movement before his rise and persisted after his death. First, it is important to recognize that Nehor insisted that his teachings were "the word of God," and though he later—under pressure—repudiated that claim, there is no evidence that his followers did likewise (Alma 1:3, 15). The most consistent religious claim within the dissenting movement was Nehor's teaching that "all mankind should be saved at the last day and that they need not fear nor tremble, but that they might lift up their heads and rejoice, for the Lord had created all men and had also redeemed all men; and in the end all men should have eternal life" (Alma 1:4). Later on we are told that the Amalekites rejected the notions of "the coming of Christ, and . . . the resurrection of the dead and that there could be no redemption for mankind save it were through the death and sufferings of Christ" because they were "after the order of the Nehors" (Alma 21:9, 4).

As has often been observed, these ideas certainly reflect universalism, the notion that all human beings are destined for heaven.[3] More, though, they reflect an optimistic vision of human nature and of earthly life. Nehor's declaration that people should "lift up their heads and rejoice" is an interesting formulation and seems echoed in the apparent marginalization of the idea of resurrection among Nephite dissenters (Alma 1:4). In Ammonihah, where, we are told, there

3. See, for instance, John L. Clark, "Painting Out the Messiah: The Theologies of Dissidents," *Journal of Book of Mormon Studies* 11/1 (2002): 16–27, as well as Dan Vogel, "Anti-Universalist Rhetoric in the Book of Mormon," in *New Approaches to the Book of Mormon*, ed. Brent Lee Metcalfe (Salt Lake City: Signature Books, 1993), 21–52.

were "many lawyers and judges and priests and teachers which were of the profession of Nehor," the resurrection seems unfamiliar, but other Nehorite ideas, such as a denial of the need for Jesus Christ, do not (Alma 14:18). The lawyer Zeezrom seems ignorant of the resurrection in Alma 12:8, for instance, asking Alma, "What does this mean which Amulek hath spoken concerning the resurrection of the dead, that all shall rise from the dead?" Antionah, a chief ruler, argues of Adam and Eve that "there was no possible chance that they should live forever" (Alma 12:21). Reconciling these ideas with Nehor's insistence that human beings would have eternal life seems a bit tricky. That may indicate that the Nephite dissenting movement was no monolith. But it also indicates that Nephite dissenters were consistently more interested in this life than in the next. For Alma, the necessity of death and the promise of resurrection fostered a right understanding of how to live: one focused not upon the mundane scrabbling each of us does to maintain our status and earn our way ahead, but upon God's ceaseless gifts of grace. For the dissenters, such ideas distracted from their aims: precisely the present-day rewards Alma sought to distract them from.

Nehor paired his optimistic vision of human life with an emphasis on material power and influence. Indeed, he particularly associates the performance of religion with getting rich: in his mind, religious leadership should be associated with economic success. He taught "that every priest and teacher had ought to become popular and they ought not to labor with their own hands, but that they had ought to be supported by the people" (Alma 1:3). The word *popular* indicates not simply that Nehor sought to amass money but also influence, and indeed he did: "Many did believe on his words, even so many that they began to support him and give him money" (Alma 1:5). This inspired Nehor to wear fine clothing—a common Book of Mormon sign of corruption—and to establish a church. After Nehor's death, leadership of his movement passed to a figure called Amlici, who was, like Nehor, "a wise man as to the wisdom of the world" (Alma 2:1). Mormon emphasizes that, like Nehor, Amlici sought influence and proved able to draw "away much people after him, even so much that they began to be very powerful" (Alma 2:2). Amlici tried to overthrow the system of elected judges and make himself a king. Mormon explicitly contrasts the monarchical Amlici movement with the elected reign of the judges, and Amlici's quest to gain power through force with "the voice of the people," over and over again (Alma 2:1–4). The contrast between Alma and Amlici is telling. While Alma, the chief judge, organizes "captains and higher captains and chief captains" to resist Amlici's military ambitions, Amlici appoints "rulers"—a word used in the book of Alma only to describe corruption: the prideful Zoramites have rulers, and the apostate Amalickiah sought to be one (Alma 2:13–14). Antionah of Ammonihah is given the title as well (Alma 12:20). Similarly, Amlici seeks to win power and enforce his religious teachings upon the Nephites with force, while Alma the Younger executed Nehor for seeking to enforce his beliefs with violence, or, as Alma put it, "thou art not only guilty of priestcraft but hast endeavored to enforce it by the sword" (Alma 2:4; 1:12). It seems apparent that the Nephite dissenting movement insisted upon conflating secular and religious authority, while Alma the Younger firmly upholds the conviction that true righteousness cannot be enforced.

The political organization of Ammonihah seems to reflect the values of Nehor and Amlici. The people of Ammonihah resist Alma's authority not because they do not believe in authority in general; rather, they do not understand Alma's authority to be relevant to them. They certainly have their own system of elites. And as with Nehor, these religious elites are those who are economically successful; indeed, in Ammonihah, religion and wealth go hand in hand. Ammonihah is the only city in the Book of Mormon in which the famous "lawyers" are present, and, like Nehor, these lawyers associate their religious doctrine with amassing wealth and power.[4] Indeed, when the Ammonihahite lawyer Zeezrom rises to engage in theological dispute with Alma and Amulek, his qualifications are given as such: "He being one of the most expert among them, having much business to do among the people" (Alma 10:31). It is no mistake this is when Mormon inserts a long discussion of Nephite currency; it is his belief that Zeezrom's theological

4. Nibley, again, associates these lawyers with sophists; John Welch, in *The Legal Cases in the Book of Mormon* (Provo, UT: Neal A. Maxwell Institute, 2008), draws distinctions between these sorts of lawyers and those in American society.

dispute is actually designed to "stir up the people" in order to "get money according to the suits which [were] brought before them; therefore they did stir up the people against Alma and Amulek" (Alma 11:20). It is this aristocracy in Ammonihah, a self-made collective reliant on individual talent and focused on material success, that seems most opposed to the preaching of Alma and Amulek.

When Alma and Amulek begin preaching in the city, then, they quickly encounter a group of people who seem committed to a set of religious beliefs that exalt the search for material success in the present at the expense of eternal life. Indeed, before Alma enters the city the first time, Mormon writes that he received a warning from an angel to the effect that the people of Ammonihah "do study at this time that they may destroy the liberty of thy people" (Alma 8:17). Alma, who was wounded in the Amlici rebellion and had surrendered political power to further spiritual success, likely had some sense of what the angel's warning might mean. Though there is little evidence for a renewed Amlicite rebellion, certainly Amlicite values had taken hold in Ammonihah, and Mormon has observed that they proved endlessly tempting.[5] In Alma 1:16 he observes that there were "many [who] loved the vain things of the world. And they went forth preaching false doctrines, and this they did for the sake of riches and honor." When Alma reaches Ammonihah, then, the people there reject him because he has resigned the judgment seat, and "we know that thou art high priest over the church which thou hast established in many parts of the land according to your tradition. And we are not of thy church" (Alma 8:11). Several verses after this, they ask him, "Who art thou? Suppose ye that we shall believe the testimony of one man, although he should preach unto us that the earth should pass away?" (Alma 9:2). Since they clearly know who Alma is, this appears a way to taunt him for his present lack of influence, rather than being an honest question. The suggestion that they are invoking the Deuteronomic law of two witnesses to truth only underscores the Ammonihahites' conviction that Alma has no formal power they are bound to respect (see Alma 9:2). Similarly, when

5. Brown, "Ammonihah: Measuring Mormon's Purposes," maintains that there was indeed a military conspiracy afoot; I am less confident in that.

Amulek speaks he makes precisely the sort of appeal we might expect: "I am also a man of no small reputation among all those who know me; yea, and behold, I have many kindred and friends. And I have also acquired much riches by the hand of my industry" (Alma 10:4). This is language the Ammonihahites, obsessed with status, might respect.

From the beginning, then, Alma and Amulek found themselves confronted with a group of people who equated the message of the church Alma represented with an attack on a social order that benefitted them. Indeed, there appears to be an essential disjuncture of understanding among Alma, Amulek, and the Ammonihahites about what precisely is at stake in their dispute. In Alma 10:24, the people of Ammonihah protest Amulek's preaching, complaining that "this man doth revile against our laws, which are just, and our wise lawyers, which we have selected." In Alma 14:5, the people echo this complaint, charging that Alma and Amulek "had reviled against the law and their lawyers and judges of the land."

Several things are interesting here. First, it is unclear exactly what laws the Ammonihahites are talking about, though a plausible reading might have them interpreting Alma and Amulek's mission as the sort of religious persecution that so recently drew such attention under Mosiah's monarchy and Alma's judgeship. Moreover, note their defense of their lawyers. They are "chosen," selected by the people in ways analogous to the choosing of the judges in Mosiah's system. But note finally that they are chosen because they are "wise," an adjective often—though not entirely—used in the book of Alma in an ironic way. Amlici is wise (Alma 2:1); the Zoramites declare they are not foolish (Alma 31:17); Nephi observes that the foolish think they are wise in 2 Nephi 9:28; and here the word seems to stand in contrast to Mosiah's desire not for "wise" but for "just men" to govern and his urging that judges in particular be "righteous" (Mosiah 29:13, 29).

Amulek denounces the people of Ammonihah as such: "Ye do not understand. Ye say that I have spoken against your law, but I have not; but I have spoken in favor of your law, to your condemnation" (Alma 10:26). It seems clear that he and they have a fundamental misunderstanding. They perceive his language about law and condemnation as an act of repression of their political and social order, and indeed the message Alma and Amulek bring would accomplish that. Amulek acknowledges this in Alma 10:27, declaring "that the foundation of the destruction of this people is . . . beginning to be laid by the unrighteousness of your lawyers and your judges," linking the spiritual failure of Ammonihah to the elites who govern the city. However, the solution Alma and Amulek offer is not political reform. Neither is it private, solitary moral reform. Rather, in Alma 12 and 13 Alma insists that a godly society requires social as well as individual moral transformation. He offers a comprehensive reframing of what Nephite society might look like: the immoral, hierarchical, meritocratic order of the Nehors supplanted with a grace-ful society in which the ultimate victories over death and fear are not earned through labor but rather accepted as a gift.

It is in this context then, that Alma's emphasis on what he calls the holy order in Alma 12–13 should be understood.[6] The lawyers of Ammonihah challenge Alma for his lack of the sort of authority they respect. In response, Alma invokes this alternative social organization: priests and people, organized "after" something called a "holy order." The phrase occurs regularly in the book of Alma, but it is first invoked when Alma resigns the judgment seat in Alma 4:20, only after Nehor has established what Mormon calls his "order" in Alma 2:1. Mormon again uses the word to describe Amlici's rebellion, which signals that we should understand Alma's holy order as not simply an ecclesiastical or spiritual affair, but a comprehensive social organization opposed to the political success of the Nephite dissenting movement. Finally, in Alma 13:1 he states, "I would that ye should remember that the Lord God ordained priests after his holy order, which was after the order of his Son, to teach these things unto the people." This holy order was a network of teachers and students, all humanity endlessly instructing their fellows in the nature of salvation.

Alma's use of the term reflects that meaning. In Zarahemla, he chastises Nephite dissenters for persecuting those who "humble

---

6. Robert Millet's "The Holy Order of God," in *The Book of Mormon: Alma, the Testimony of the Word*, ed. Monte S. Nyman and Charles D. Tate Jr. (Provo, UT: Religious Studies Center, Brigham Young University, 1992), 61–88, argues that the holy order is a reference to ordinance work, specifically ordination to the Melchizedek Priesthood and temple rites.

themselves and do walk after the holy order of God wherewith they have been brought into this church" (Alma 5:54). When Alma resigns the judgment seat, Mormon claims that he "confined himself wholly to the high priesthood of the holy order of God" in order to "reclaim" the people from "pride and craftiness" (Alma 4:19–20). This can be seen as a reference to "priestcraft," the crime for which Alma executed Nehor, which Mormon defines as "preaching . . . for the sake of riches and honor" (Alma 1:16). Mormon uses the phrase *holy order* to refer to Alma's commission; Alma himself invokes the phrase to describe the priest's requirement to go out to teach; it is also, apparently, a way of life. Rather than the priestcraft of the dissenting movement, which associates correct religious leadership with economic gain, Alma presents them with a way of life premised on the egalitarian reception of grace.

In his discourse in response to Antionah, Alma describes the production of the holy order as a series of gifts, from God to humanity, from one set of human beings to another. God "sent" angels to humanity in order to inspire them to reach out to God. Then God "made known unto them the plan of redemption"; then God "gave unto them commandments." Finally, God established the "holy order" by calling priests "to teach these things unto the people." These series of exchanges are not premised upon skill or talent or effort: rather, they are a matter of giving and receiving in gratitude (Alma 12:29–32; 13:1). Alma then echoes biblical language used in Psalms and the Epistle to the Hebrews, warning the people of Ammonihah against the "provocation" that the children of Israel committed against God in the exodus. Fearing that they could not successfully occupy the land of Israel, the children of Israel doubted God's gifts and complained that they would rather return to the grinding regularity of slavery in Egypt, where work was consistently, if meagerly, rewarded, rather than trust in the unpredictability of grace (Exodus 17). This is, of course, what the Ammonihahites have done: though they profess faith in God, their actions show that their true faith is in the reliability of their own talents rather than in the seeming mysterious promises of God.

Finally, Alma invokes Melchizedek. As previously, Alma's language echoes two biblical passages describing this mysterious figure: that of Genesis and that of Hebrews. Hebrews emphasizes Melchizedek's own righteousness, praising him as, "without father, without mother, without descent, having neither beginning of days, nor end of life; but made like unto the Son of God." Melchizedek is a figure without human connection and thus of great authority. In Hebrews as in Genesis, Melchizedek receives tithes from Abraham, and the author of Hebrews enjoins us to "consider how great this man was, unto whom even the patriarch Abraham gave the tenth of the spoils" (Hebrews 7:3–4).

But Alma's telling reorients the story. His emphasis is not on Melchizedek's righteousness but rather on the transformation of his kingdom, the people of Salem, who are at the beginning of the narrative horribly wicked. Alma observes not simply that Melchizedek "received the office of the high priesthood according to the holy order of God" but also that Melchizedek reigns under the guidance of his father. Moreover, Alma presents Melchizedek as a man similar to himself, as a king who receives priestly office and thereupon seeks to preach to his people and guide them to repentance rather than enforcing righteousness. And, as Alma hopes to be, Melchizedek's preaching is successful: the people repent when they hear Melchizedek's words. This process worked to "establish peace in the land" (Alma 13:16–18). In Alma's telling of the story, the relationship between Melchizedek and his people is the primary focus, a relationship premised on persuasion rather than on power. Indeed, it stands as an example of what the holy order is: a community of mutual service, in which Melchizedek receives priestly authority in order to minister to his people; his triumph is not of power or wealth but of conversions gained.

Alma says twice that peace is the real prize of Melchizedek's holy order (Alma 13:18). Peace is something that the people of Ammonihah—and indeed, the Nephite dissenting movement as a whole—distinctly lack. In Mosiah 27, which describes the waning years of the reign of Mosiah, the dissenting movement rises in power, and the result is murmuring, complaining, and persecution within the church as well as without (Mosiah 27:1–2). The restoration of peace, we are told, comes only when Mosiah pleads with his people that "they should let no pride nor haughtiness disturb their peace, that every man should esteem his neighbor as himself, laboring with their own hands for their support" (Mosiah 27:4). And it is only then, we are told, that "there began to be much peace again in the land" (Mosiah 27:6). It is precisely this sort of society that Alma believes in, and it is the structure behind his Melchizedek narrative. The holy order, then, is to Alma more than simply a church or a priesthood—it is a righteous society. The Nephite dissenting movement is more than simply a theological challenge—it is a disordered society. In the last analysis, then, the people of Ammonihah were correct: Alma did seek to overthrow their laws. He did so, though, because to him, right belief and right society were inseparable.

Conversing and Calling in Alma 12 and 13

David Charles Gore

THEOLOGY, Θεός–λογία OR *THEOS-LOGIA*, contains within itself notions of composition, collaboration, conversing, and calling. Theology is an invitation to commune. However, the study of communication theology remains relatively neglected. We might understand communication theology as the use of media and other means of disseminating messages for theological purposes, but, like Franz-Josef Eilers, I intend something broader.[1] Communication is central to who God is and what God does; God is a communicating being. By placing communication at the center of theology, something implied by the *-logos* etymology, we can find communication in who God is (i.e., the Godhead), how he reveals his nature to human beings (i.e., revelation), how we participate in being by way of communication (i.e., embodiment), and what it means to belong to a social body that is engaged in communicative practices (i.e., the church).[2] The magnetism of communication is

1. I am indebted to Franz-Josef Eilers for giving me the language to sort through what a theology of communication might look like. See his "Communication Theology: Some Considerations," http://www.freinademetzcenter.org/pdf/Communication_Theology.pdf.

2. See Eilers, "Communication Theology," 3. I have borrowed his ideas but changed his language to move it from a Catholic to a Mormon context, but the basic concepts of his theology of communication are relayed.

embedded in its etymological root word: the Latin *munus* conveys the idea of making things common, as especially in a common room or shared space; it has an additional connotation of a gift.[3] The essence of theology and religious living is found in learning how to receive gifts and how to share gifts with others.

Elements of communication theology, including conversing, calling, and sharing gifts, characterize the sermon Alma delivers to the people of Ammonihah in response to Antionah's questions. The people of Ammonihah are depicted as revilers, easily angered, ready to lay hands on others, and driven by popularity, power, and money—especially money (see Alma 8:13; 9:7; 11:20, 24; 14:7–8). Antionah's questions are about death and the possibilities of resurrection. In response, Alma preaches of a God who "made known . . . the plan of redemption," who "called with a holy calling," and established an order "in a manner that thereby the people might know in what manner to look forward to his son for redemption" (Alma 12:30; 13:3, 2). What was the process whereby God "made known" his plan and "called with a holy calling"? Unmistakably, this process is communicative in nature and reveals a God motivated to share existence with us and to summon us to his way of being. The context of Alma's sermon and the reality of death and judgment that Alma insists upon give shape to God's communicative motivations in conversing and calling upon his children and making known the gifts he has always already given.

The rhetorical context: I was about to explain!

The rhetorical exchange between Antionah and Alma begins with Antionah's eighty-seven-word *hypophora*—a rhetorical device in which a speaker raises a question and promptly answers it.[4] We cannot know

---

3. See the discussion of Gisbert Greshake's work in Eilers, "Communication Theology," 1.

4. *Hypophora* refers to the dissenting statement or question and *anthypophora* refers to the answer. The two terms have come to be exchangeable as embracing both elements, according to Wikipedia, s.v. "Hypophora," https://en.wikipedia.org/wiki/Hypophora. The figure need not always be seen as disingenuous, as it is often employed as a kind of reasoning aloud. See Gideon O. Burton, "anthypophora," Silva Rhetoricae,

for sure whether Antionah's questions were asked sincerely or as a provocation to or for the crowd. We do know that the lawyers, judges, and rulers at Ammonihah, of which Antionah was a "chief ruler," were known for stirring up "the people to riotings and all manner of disturbances and wickedness" (Alma 11:20). Indeed, directly following Alma's sermon, a wave of violence hits this community, which may have been part of Antionah's intention (see Alma 14). The fact that Antionah answers his own questions with an assertion delivered with categorical certainty suggests he is not giving Alma a real hearing, but some in the crowd obviously are inclined to listen to and to be persuaded by Alma (Alma 14:1–2). That Antionah's questions show familiarity with the scriptures raises issues about how familiar the audience at Ammonihah is with the writings of scripture and with engagement and debate about theological questions.

Alma seems unfazed by any provocation and responds to Antionah's inquiry with the enthusiastic explanation, "I was about to explain" (Alma 12:22). Alma takes Antionah's questions seriously, at least with respect to the immediate audience at Ammonihah, and addresses them with a 1,645-word discursive, sermonic response. If the text we have is accurate and we assume an average English-speaking rate of 130 words per minute, this entire exchange would have taken about thirteen and a half minutes to deliver publicly. This microsermon is part of a larger series of exchanges that includes sermons by Amulek and Alma, questions and discussion from the audience, including especially lengthy exchanges between Zeezrom and Amulek and between Zeezrom and Alma, as well as words we do not have (Alma 9–14; 9:34; 13:31). If we take only the words recorded in the text, the whole exchange could have been performed in just under an hour. Most likely it took longer, given that there are words, perhaps even entire paragraphs, missing. We do not know if these exchanges all took place on a single day, but it was certainly possible for that to have been the case.

---

http://rhetoric.byu.edu/Figures/A/anthypophora.htm. A reading that discredits Antionah is one rooted largely in *ethos*—we know that he is a "ruler" and that the answer he provides to the question runs contrary to Alma's claims.

Antionah's questions and declarative statement as well as Alma's sermon have the appearance of spontaneous, digressive call and response. Echoing scriptural passages found in Genesis, Psalms, and Hebrews, the sermon does not read like a carefully reasoned, deliberately composed theological argument. Instead it has the makings of a live composition of assertions, claims, and beliefs touching on a range of topics from the fall of "our first parents," the resurrection, the meaning of "the plan of redemption," the centrality of the heart, and the calling and ordination of priests. Taken together, what seems like it would be a jumble actually has a consistent message that revolves around the plan of redemption as a means of preparing the people to "look forward on the son of God . . . for a remission of their sins" (Alma 13:16). In order to make this point stick, Alma addresses how death gives shape to life and how judgment gives shape to life after death.

Pending appointments: They must die and they must come to judgment

Not only does Antionah suggest that death is the end, but his questions imply that it was never part of God's plan that we should live forever. Questioning Amulek and Alma's account of the resurrection, Antionah makes specific reference to the fall of our first parents, at which point God blocked the way to the tree of life by armed cherubims. Antionah asks, in essence, "How is resurrection possible if God blocked the way to the tree of life from the beginning?"

Alma admits straightaway that by our first parents partaking of the fruit "all mankind became a lost and a fallen people" (Alma 12:22).[5] In short, Alma agrees that God appointed us to die. Where he differs with Antionah is that he does not see death as the end. To make this case, Alma disassociates physical death, what many consider to be the worst that can happen, from what Alma has already referred to in response to Zeezrom as "spiritual death" (Alma 12:16). *Temporal death* and *second*

5. *A lost and a fallen* as well as *lost and fallen* are not phrases appearing in the KJV. In fact, it is remarkable how many phrases in these chapters have a KJV ring to them but in fact do not appear there.

death become phrases Alma uses to distinguish between the death of the body and the more alarming death of the spirit. This distinction leads to a discussion of a space that intervenes between physical death and spiritual death, which is characterized by judgment that may result in a permanent separation of one's spirit from God (Alma 12:24, 32). "It was appointed unto man that they must die. And after death they must come to judgment, even that same judgment . . . which is the end" (Alma 12:27).

Now, if both of these appointments were to happen in the same moment—as would have happened if our first parents ate the fruit of both trees in the garden—there would have been no opportunity for an intervention between our physical and spiritual deaths. There could have been no time to prepare to meet God, no time to comprehend the role of the Savior, no time to repent.

But it was not given to us that we should live forever in our sins. Instead, "there was a space granted unto man in which he might repent" (Alma 12:24). We need not dwell forever in our rebellion against ourselves. We need not forever tear ourselves up over our inadequacies, our shortcomings, our failures to hit the target, our willful disobedience, our straying thoughts, our lustful eyes, our weak wills, our pride, hateful and spiteful words, impatience, unholiness, unkindness, bitterness, dishonesty, mean-spiritedness, and viciousness. None of this will live forever because we die—and all of this can be redeemed because we have a Savior.

Alma speaks of a faith whereby sin is not definitive, of a life that is a preparation, and of a death that is not the end. By framing death as something given, appointed, and as the end of preparation, Alma places the focus on life, on what we do in the here and now. Instead of thinking about life as our one chance to get our own, to think and act for ourselves, to get ahead, to look good, to become popular and powerful, life is "a probationary state, a time to prepare to meet God" (Alma 12:24). The manner in which we are to prepare, it will be shown, is after the order of the Son of God. The law is the law, but probation enacts a state of space, a state of grace, between the law and its punishment. It is granted to us that we die; in the meantime, it is granted to us to live, but to live in a state of preparation.

There are two things, Alma says, for which we must prepare: prepare to meet God and "prepare for that endless state" (Alma 12:24). That endless state may be a life with God or a life without God. Regardless, whether we believe in God or no God, we all must confront the possibility of some endless state in front of us. Life now is a preparatory state of some kind, even if we do not know with certainty what we are preparing for. Before we can eat the fruit of the tree of life we must prepare ourselves. What else is life but a getting ready? Every day we prepare. Ready or not, every day comes at us, and then the night. We can run from our conscience, waste our time, riot and rage, or simply whimper and whine, but an end is coming, an end that is endless. Every day of our life is lived in preparation for that endless state, whether we like it or not, whether we admit it or not, whether we get ready or not.

Whereas Antionah thinks death is the end, Alma believes judgment is the end. This shift in register moves the conversation from death to life. Antionah has, apparently, no conception of a second appointment or final reckoning. He thinks only of the first, of the death of his body. This smaller perspective constrains the horizon of what is possible in mortal time. Alma, on the other hand, wants to show Antionah and the people of Ammonihah how to see mortal time as a preparation. The images of probation and judgment tell us something about who we are and what we are like, that perhaps we are not readily to be trusted. That seems to be the humility of the religious impulse, which is different from the pride of one seeking to highlight contradiction in the religious life of others or in scripture or setting power and gain in the short run over every other consideration.

Communicating the plan: It was expedient that man should know

After having appointed us to death and judgment, God then set up a process to prepare us for death and judgment. The process whereby God informs us is manifold and includes the ministering of angels, prayer, conversing with men, and calling humankind to faith and repentance through the gift of his Son. God summons us, commissions us, and names us, in and through Christ.

The process of making known the plan of redemption as outlined in Alma's sermon includes the following steps:

1. The ministering of angels (Alma 12:29)
2. Men "behold[ing] of his glory" and "call[ing] on his name" (Alma 12:29–30)
3. "God convers[ing] with men . . . in the name of his Son" about "the plan of redemption" (Alma 12:30, 33)
4. "God ordain[ing] priests after . . . the order of his Son, to teach these things unto the people" (Alma 13:1)

It was expedient that the plan be made known in order for us to comprehend ourselves and our existence. As angels converse with humanity, humanity begins to understand God's nature and to converse with him through prayer. In response to these prayers, God converses with those who turn to him in faith. These are then called and sanctified and sent forth to teach and preach.

The process of making known the things of God is one that is recounted again and again in the scriptures. The phrase *made known* occurs thirty-six times in the Book of Mormon, with six occurrences in Alma 12 and 13, three of which are in verses 28 and 32. Half of all uses of this phrase, eighteen, occur in the book of Alma. By contrast, the phrase *made known* occurs twenty-two times in the KJV.[6] The Book of Mormon phrase does not appear sacrosanct, as it is used to describe the sharing of secret combinations by both Kishkumen and Akish, but the vast majority of Book of Mormon references employ the phrase in conjunction with God, Jesus, the Holy Ghost, and angels who made known the details of their work. The only references to things made known in connection with angels are by Alma, save one reference by King Benjamin, who says that the things in his great sermon were made known to him by an angel (Mosiah 3:2). Alma's sermon at Zarahemla in Alma 5 included things made known by the Holy Spirit of God after much fasting and prayer (Alma 5:46). To the people of Gideon,

---

6. The Book of Mormon includes seven times the phrase *make known*; the KJV twenty-five.

Alma perceived that the nature of God had been made known by the testimony of his word (Alma 7:20).

Alma's contemporary, King Mosiah's son Ammon, identifies a similar pattern as that described by Alma in his response to Antionah. Thus Ammon reports:

> And the great God has had mercy on us and made these things known unto us that we might not perish. Yea, and he hath made these things known unto us beforehand because he loveth our souls as well as he loveth our children. Therefore, in his mercy he doth visit us by his angels, that the plan of salvation might be made known unto us as well as unto future generations. (Alma 24:14)

The plan set in motion by God moves according to his love and mercy—for us and our children. Our salvation and its being made known is a matter that brings families together through generations of time and saves us "that we might not perish." The terms *beforehand* and *future* suggest that the process operates through all of time. "God made known" is a trope for both Alma and Ammon, a way of describing a process that operates through love, mercy, and angels. Their shared reference to this process suggests they may have discussed it together. It was certainly something they both were teaching.

The only occurrence in the KJV of the phrase *made known* with any connection to angels is in Luke 2, the familiar story of angels announcing Jesus's birth:

> And it came to pass, as the angels were gone away from them into heaven, the shepherds said one to another, Let us now go even unto Bethlehem, and see this thing which is come to pass, which the Lord hath made known unto us. And they came with haste, and found Mary, and Joseph, and the babe lying in a manger. And when they had seen it, they made known abroad the saying which was told them concerning this child. (Luke 2:15–17)

This story conforms to the pattern outlined by Alma. To wit, angels converse with shepherds, the shepherds respond by coming to Christ and literally beholding of his glory, they then "make known abroad" what the angels had said about this holy child. God calls to his children by angels, his children turn to him and behold his glory, and they then turn to one another and "make known the saying." There are echoes of this story when Alma declares "glad tidings of great joy" and prophesies that the gospel will be "made known . . . in plain terms" and "made known unto just and holy men," possibly the very same shepherds just mentioned (see Alma 13:23, 26). For Alma, the process of making known includes "anxiety" and "pain," but ultimately one that he hopes will yield repentance (Alma 13:27–30).

The account of the process of things made known by Alma is unique in all of scripture because Alma tells us that "God conversed with men" (Alma 12:30). The words *converse* and *conversed* appear six times altogether in the Book of Mormon, all in connection with angels except for Alma 12:30 (see Alma 9:21; 12:29–30; 19:34; Helaman 5:38–39). Alma 12:30 is the only place where we are told that God conversed. Other scriptures make wide use of *converse* and *conversation*, and reference to these uses will aid us in grasping the wide meaning available for this concept and for comprehending how it is that God converses. Curiously the word *converse* does not appear in the KJV.[7] The word *conversation*, on the other hand, shows up at several different places and under several different guises.

The first place is under the Hebrew verb *derek*, which is often translated "way," "toward," "journey," and "manner."[8] (Incidentally *derek* is the verb in Genesis 3:24 where the "cherubims" and the flaming sword "*keep the way* of the tree of life" [emphasis added].) In the Psalms, the same verb appears as "communication."[9] Four Greek terms are also translated as "communication" or "communicate" in the New Testament:

7. It does appear in the deuterocanonical books of Baruch 3:37 and Bel and the Dragon 1:2.

8. Strong's H1870.

9. Psalms 37:14 and 50:23.

1. *Politeuma* (Strong's G4176), translated as "conversation" only in Philippians; it has associations with political community and citizenship.[10]
2. *Tropos* (Strong's G5158), meaning "as," "in like manner," translated "communication" at Hebrews 13:5.
3. *Anastrephō* and *anastrophe* (Strong's G390 and G391), meaning "manner of life," "conduct," "behavior," "deportment," with the former carrying also the meaning of "to overturn," "abide," "behave," "conversation," "overthrow," and "turn upside down." This verb is used to show Jesus overturning the tables of the money changers in the temple. Paul uses it to denote our conversation with the world and our conversation with the old man, our former self, before repentance.[11] The books of 1 and 2 Peter make wide use of the term translated "conversation" to encourage us to strive after holy and honest conversation in Christ and to avoid the "conversation" of the wicked.
4. *Koinōneō* (G2841), translated as "distributing," "partaking," "sharing," and "communicate."[12]

The first thing that should be apparent from this list is the wide range of associations available for the concept of conversation. Much broader than the conveyance of information, the term must be recognized as including something akin to a mode and manner of life. The emphasis in the New Testament is clearly placed on conversation as a means of carrying ourselves in preparation for Christ's return. To communicate means to share things in common. Conversation can be seen in terms of behaving and conducting oneself in a manner that overturns the ordinary course of things and behavior. Nowhere does the KJV use the term *conversation* to describe God's interactions with humankind, so it may be no wonder then that non-Mormon Christians may hold

10. Philippians 1:27 and 3:20.
11. In Ephesians 2:3 and 4:22; James 3:13 uses it to describe Christian conversation.
12. See Galatians 6:6 and Philippians 4:15: "communicate" and "communicated with."

different conceptions of what it means to communicate with God than those held by believers in the Book of Mormon.

We have already discussed that angels "caused men to behold of his glory," but when God conversed he "made known unto them the plan of redemption . . . and this he made known unto them according to their faith and repentance and their holy works" (Alma 12:29–30). God "gave unto them commandments *after* having made known unto them the plan of redemption, that they should not do evil, the penalty thereof being a second death" (v. 32). God's conversations are always in the context of what he has prepared for our redemption. It was in these conversations that God "did call on men in the name of his Son" (v. 33). God wants us to become acquainted with him, and his conversations with us can be seen as a kind of test as they come "according to" a formula of "faith, repentance, and holy works." It appears that God is deliberate in the sequencing of his messages to us and that he reserved for himself the opportunity of making known the plan of redemption: it was God who introduced his Son to the world and gave to his children commandments that they should not do evil. The sequencing of these revelations is significant because it shows a desire to prepare us, to help us grow.

While it is no doubt crucial *what* God communicates, it is also crucial *that* God communicates. Love and mercy are expressed in large part by communicating in the first place, by opening a conversation in which we come to feel comfortable participating. Every message contains informational as well as relational content. As often happens, the latter speaks louder than the former and has longer-lasting consequences. Central to Mormonism and to Alma's sermon is the claim that God has, does, and will communicate the details of his plan to his children—a plan of mercy, redemption, and salvation. Without downplaying the significance of the details and content of what God communicates, it is important to note that God is engaging in a process with us. The point of this process is to develop a relationship whereby we prepare ourselves to enter the divine presence.

Conversation is one of the ways we gain acquaintance with others and whereby they become familiar to us. Conversation builds and reinforces relationships. By exchanging thoughts, opinions, and feelings, we come to grasp where other people are coming from and gain insight to their hearts. Conversation with friends is one of the great joys of life and perhaps ought to become the standard set for our dealings with God—as the example of Abraham indicates. For many, however, conversing with God, through living and praying, can sometimes be agonizing as we work our way through processes of faithlessness and the stages of repentance. The upshot of these conversations is hopefully to come to a greater understanding of his love for us and to gain greater acceptance of our status as children and heirs. It is a rare thing for us to talk about revelation in terms of conversation, but the idea that God wants to be in communication with us should be a comforting one. The Latin root of *converse* means literally "to turn," as in a turn to face each other or the taking of turns in conversation. This has connotations for conversion, which is likewise a turning. The turning of conversation includes a coming together, as in an embrace or a dance.

Consider, for example, the unbroken chain of conversation inside our own heads with which we are all familiar. Psychologists refer to this as "inner speech" and demonstrated nearly a century ago that when we speak to ourselves there are tiny muscular movements in the larynx. In the 1990s, neuroscientists showed that Broca's area of the brain, the left inferior frontal gyrus, becomes active during both inner and outer speech. This internal conversation, which is both physical and psychological, indicates a potential division of the self—as we speak to ourselves and listen to ourselves at the same time. The running conversation in our heads is always personal and often enough selfish and self-absorbed. It can even verge on the terrifying as we find ourselves thinking and saying things that we would be horrified to give audible voice to or enact in real life. This inner speech can be a running argument with ourselves, but it can also verge into an argument with God. At the same time, this ongoing dialogue we have with ourselves about life's situations, difficulties, and graces can also become a form of prayer as our thoughts turn Godward. I am suggesting that this inner dialogue, just like the rest of us, may be redeemed. However cynical or self-absorbed our conversations with ourselves or others have become, they await a judgment that will be given in mercy and love.

David Hume, one of the world's great conversationalists who treated the topic in his *Essays,* was always ready for an easy and agreeable conversation. He claimed that the true measure of the value of knowing a thing was whether anyone wanted to talk about it. Hume's desire to keep conversation easy and agreeable would perhaps clash with the conversation Alma had with the angel, in which he was spoken to by the voice of thunder. Even though some conversations with God and angels may not always be easy and agreeable, these conversations should always be seen as possible and desirable—Alma certainly came to see his conversation with the angel in these terms (Alma 36:5–6, 20). The notion of God conversing with us invites the possibility of a more approachable, more colloquial way of thinking and talking about talking with God.

What might we better grasp about God if we spoke of all forms of conversation and communication as potentially revelatory? How might our conversations with others be enriched by imagining them as "the Gods [taking] counsel among themselves" (Abraham 4:26)? When I was an anxious young graduate student, my advisor reassured me by suggesting I imagine myself participating in a conversation that started long before I was born and will stretch on long after I'm gone. I found this both encouraging and enchanting—one can never grasp all that has been thought and said in the world, but one may nevertheless realize that, though having joined a conversation late, one can still claim a turn. The idea of having a conversation is so ordinary and so commonplace that it should not intimidate anyone. To think of ourselves in conversation with God should reassure us and help us in imagining an approachable God. To see each of our conversations with one another as a grand and cosmic conversation in microcosm can elevate these everyday interactions to a higher plane. Terryl Givens comes close to a conception of revelation as conversing with his term *dialogic revelation,*[13] but we must not place the emphasis solely on words and content. Our conversation with God should be seen in terms of an ongoing relationship that includes gestures, thoughts, wailing, gnashing of

---

13. See Terryl Givens, *By the Hand of Mormon: The American Scripture That Launched a New World Religion* (Oxford: Oxford University Press, 2002).

teeth, the pulling of hair and the rending of clothes, moods, fears, anxieties, groaning, singing, dancing, praising, mourning, and tears. Especially tears. Just as in our conversations with other people, we will be, by turns, enlightened, frustrated, upset, challenged, invited, and persuaded by conversing with God.

Called with a holy calling

Nevertheless, we must keep in mind that conversing with God can often lead to attachments, expectations, and obligations. Indeed, God not only converses with us, but he also calls us, calls upon us, and calls us to call to others. What does it mean to be "called *with* a holy calling," to be "called *to* this holy calling," and to be "called *by* this holy calling" (Alma 13:3–4, 6)? Why the repetition of *called* and *calling*? Why alter the phrasing, using *with*, *to*, and *by*?

We can readily establish that *holy* in Webster's 1828 Dictionary indicates wholeness and perfection in a moral sense. Webster adds "pure in heart, temper, or dispositions," then contrasts the holiness of the Supreme Being with the holiness of men, stating that God's holiness "is perfectly pure, immaculate, and complete," whereas man is more or less *holy* as his heart is more or less sanctified, or purified from evil dispositions. We call a man *holy* when his heart is conformed in some degree to the image of God, and his life is regulated by the divine precepts. Hence, *holy* is used as nearly synonymous with *good*, *pious*, *godly*.

Straightaway we gain a conception of holiness operating in two registers, divine and human. And then, just as with Alma, we see that holiness for men is a question of the heart—whether it is more or less sanctified and "conformed in some degree to the image of God." Webster has all of this down without reference to the Book of Mormon. What is Alma adding?

To be called, beckoned to, or addressed from across a gap implies God's longing for us to be with him. God desires to close the space between us. Implicated in being called and receiving a calling are associations having to do with being repeatedly visited and solicited. Alma seems to be struggling to articulate how to account for this holy calling. Its privileges apparently rest on both grace and agency. Those "having chosen good and exercising exceeding great faith are called with a holy calling" (Alma 13:3). In the next verse they are "called to this holy calling," and two verses later they are "called by this holy calling." Thus, in Alma, we encounter the following formulations:

1. A summons: "They having chosen good and exercising exceeding great faith *are called with a holy calling*" (13:3, and repeated in 13:8).
2. A commission: "Thus they *having been called to this holy calling* on account of their faith" (13:4).
3. A naming: "And thus *being called by this holy calling* and ordained unto the high priesthood of the holy order of God" (13:6).

To be "called with" could refer to God's beckoning or summoning. To be "called to" could refer to a commission to an office, empowered to take action. To be "called by" could refer to naming—we must be called by the name of Christ to be saved. "Being called by this holy calling" could also have reference to the ways in which the office or order functions as a call to others, inviting them to likewise repent, harden not their hearts, and consider the blindness of their minds. Earlier, Alma noted that humankind is called "*to call on* his name," the name of Christ (12:30).

Being called with, to, and by a calling suggests that not everything can depend on us since we cannot call ourselves. We must hear the call, be ready to respond, respond, and then be changed because of the call—all the while hardening not our hearts. Whatever role we play pales in comparison to the calling of God and his Son. It is we who are called upon and visited. That the call is "prepared from the foundation of the world according to the foreknowledge of God" suggests it is part of God's process put in motion long before our birth (Alma 13:3). The division of agency in 12:31 of our parents both placing themselves and being placed in a state to act persists in this language as Alma tries to reconnoiter and express the dimensions of this "holy calling." There are many different ways to express God's calling upon his children, and each of them can aid us in understanding our relationship with God and the manner in which he cultivates and develops that relationship with us.

The calling came first to Christ and then through Christ to all of us. It was "prepared from the foundation of the world for such as would not harden their hearts" and exists "in and through the atonement of the Only Begotten Son which was prepared" (Alma 13:5). The call's long preparation and association with the atonement means that it is not possible to be called or to respond appropriately to the call without a Savior. We are called with the name of Christ, called to the name of Christ, and called by the name of Christ. "This high priesthood [is] after the order of his Son which order was from the foundation of the world" (Alma 13:7). Hardness of heart, blindness of mind, vanity of heart, unfaithfulness, and "the crafts of men" all form obstacles in the way of being called with, to, and by this holy calling. While we frequently read these verses as emphasizing the righteousness of those who are called, it is that Alma speaks first and foremost of the righteousness of the Lamb—the calling and slaying of Jesus from the foundation of the world—as the essence of being called.

Conclusion

It is obvious that Alma is witnessing his own relationship with God and angels in the short sermon that bridges Alma 12 and 13. This relationship was a tumultuous one, filled with rebellion, pain, repentance, anxiety, success, failure, suffering, and joy. Much like the manner in which we live, Alma was engaging in a process with God, the process of coming to accept and live after a particular manner. To see ourselves in conversation with God and as called with, to, and by God is to recognize our kinship with God (and with Alma). To be called is to understand that one's life has a purpose and a becoming beyond itself. It is to recognize one's kinship with God and other people. "God did call on men," and he did so because of his mercy and his love. He wants us to partake of his rest. Working our way there means coming to terms with our probationary state, living fully within the space granted in which we "prepare to meet God" and "prepar[ing] for that endless state . . . which is after the resurrection" (Alma 12:24). The mechanism of this preparation is fundamentally communicative. We must learn how to live within God's order by learning to accept that which God is always already giving. We must learn to live in a manner that shows our willingness to learn from God, to converse and to listen, to suffer correction and to pray, to call and be called.

Angels and a Theology of Grace

Rosemary Demos

Embedded in Alma's sermon to the people of Ammonihah is a short and cryptic narrative. A brief glimpse of interactions between God, angels, and men, it is at best a brief outline of a story. Alma identifies no characters by name, establishes no time or place, and adds no poetic embellishments. The entire sequence takes up only a few verses. Yet it is a crucial turning point in the theology of his discourse. Before these verses, Alma has described God's foreknowledge and humanity's creation and fall. But he continues:

> [God] saw that it was expedient that man should know concerning the things whereof he had appointed unto them. Therefore he sent angels to converse with them, which caused men to behold of his glory. And they began from that time forth to call on his name; therefore God conversed with men and made known unto them the plan of redemption which had been prepared from the foundation of the world. And this he made known unto them according to their faith and repentance and their holy works. (Alma 12:28–30)

Pivoting on these verses, Alma's sermon turns away from a description of divine omniscience and toward an explication of human processes of learning. While God's divine design for his creation may be said to precede history itself, it is only at this moment that his plan is actualized. Time has been set in motion, and the eternal plan of redemption now requires human awareness, understanding, and cooperation.

Throughout Alma's sermon in chapters 12 and 13, God and mortals (both as a collective humanity and as individuals like Melchizedek) alternate as protagonists. However, Alma 12:28–30 inserts an unforeseen third group of characters: angels are sent to manifest God's glory to humanity. In this scenario, angels are *not* primarily informative messengers or administrators of the law or commandments. Although the text uses the word *converse*, this term does not necessarily indicate even an exchange of words. The primary definition for *converse* in the 1828 Webster's dictionary is "to keep company, to associate, to cohabit"[1]—not to engage in a verbal dialogue. With this sequence of interactions, angelic manifestations of glory are juxtaposed with the subsequent establishment of laws or commandments, given as instruction by God himself. This counterintuitive distinction identifies angels with glory and God himself with understated but informative communication.

But an insistent narrative ambiguity raises theological questions as well. Is Alma describing an already-familiar story? Is he retelling a specific narrative from Old World Hebrew scripture or perhaps from his own people's scriptural history? Is he instead setting forth a spiritual or symbolic narrative that could or should be likened to individual personal experience?

These questions cannot be answered by the three verses themselves. Taken alone, Alma 12:28–30 is ostensibly free of literary allusions or narrative detail, but in fact this narrative does *not* stand alone. It is embedded within a densely populated landscape of stories, character profiles, and poetic diction and should be considered within that context. Alma's discourse to the Ammonihahites (Alma 12–13) is not only theologically complex but also densely intertextual, rich with allusions to both Old and New World scriptural traditions. Within his sermon, Alma introduces his hearers to refigured biblical figures such as Melchizedek and Adam, along with retellings of familiar stories

1. *American Dictionary of the English Language*, online ed., s.v. "converse," http://webstersdictionary1828.com/Dictionary/converse.

from varied sources. Considered within the literary framework of these chapters, the brief sequence of Alma 12:28–30 can unfold into four distinct narrative possibilities, each one emerging out of these same few verses but telling a slightly different story of angels and glory. With such varied interpretive possibilities, Alma's passage prompts us not only to read deeply but also to read from varied perspectives. With each added narrative perspective, we can see a richly layered theology of an angelic commission of glory and its preparatory function within the plan of redemption.

The following analysis focuses on these multiple interpretive possibilities. The questions I will address for each narrative scenario are simple: Who are angels? What is glory? And how do angels and glory function within the subsequent establishment of God's holy order?

The fall: Adam and Eve's angelic encounter

First, let's situate Alma's discourse within the context of his dialogue with the Ammonihahite ruler, Antionah. In Alma 12:21, Antionah cites the story of Adam and Eve in his interrogation of Alma: "What does this scripture mean which saith that God placed cherubims and a flaming sword on the east of the garden of Eden lest our first parents should enter and partake of the fruit of the tree of life and live forever?" Alma responds with direct references to Adam (see 12:22–23) and "our first parents" (12:26), as he insists that death is necessary within God's plan of redemption. It is possible therefore to read his subsequent narrative of God's communications with man as a simple continuation of his retelling of this Genesis story, still a direct response to Antionah's question. If we fill in the gaps in Alma 12:29–30 with details from the Genesis account, we can annotate Alma's narrative verses thus:

> Therefore he [God] sent angels [cherubim] to converse with them [our first parents], which caused men to behold of his glory [the flaming sword]. And they [Adam and Eve] began from that time forth to call on his name; therefore God conversed with men and made known

> unto them the plan of redemption which had been prepared from the foundation of the world.

Who are the angels, and what is the glory in this story? As angelic messengers, the cherubim stand as guardians of the necessary boundary between life and death. In this story, the glory of the Lord, the cherubim's flaming sword, is both a threatening and a protective force. A punishing consequence of their transgression in the Garden of Eden, the cherubim and flaming sword cut Adam and Eve off from the presence of God and enforce the penalty of death. But this enforced mortality simultaneously gives the human race a chance to receive the law. Confronted with the wrathful glory of the cherubim, Adam and Eve call upon God for mercy and receive instructions from the Lord. Their subsequent dialogue with God is narrated in the Pearl of Great Price, where in Moses 5:4–5, the Lord responds to their cries with commandments, preparing them for a clearer understanding of the plan of redemption.

When Alma 12:28–30 is read within the context of the Genesis origin story, Alma's narrative clarifies the beginnings of human history and demonstrates that the angelic revelation of glory was a necessary preface to the ordered structure of God's subsequent commandments. This manifestation of glory (in this instance as a wrathful flaming sword) ensured the preparatory state of mortality, without which humanity "would have been forever miserable" (Alma 12:26).

The exodus: Angels among the Israelites

But Alma's brief sequence does not name Adam and Eve specifically. And its use of the more generalized "men" rather than "Adam" or "first parents" can point listeners and readers to a different biblical narrative. Indeed, as Alma continues in later verses, he makes clear allusions to the exodus story. Within Alma 12:35–37, Alma cites the first and last "provocation" and warns the people of being barred from the "rest" of the Lord. His diction mirrors that of Jacob 1, Hebrews 3, and Psalm 95, all three chapters that explicitly reference the Israelites' forty years of wandering in the wilderness.[2] Alma's layering of this exodus story on top of the Genesis narrative gives us another possible setting for an angelic manifestation of glory. The angels of the exodus take on a somewhat different role than the cherubim with flaming sword. Here angels are not clearly personified agents; instead, the use of the term is merged with descriptions of the raw manifestation of divine power. Indeed, Moses's early dialogue with the Lord is preceded by an angel whose embodiment seems to be the miracle of the burning bush itself: "And the angel of the Lord appeared unto him in a flame of fire out of the midst of a bush: and he looked, and, behold, the bush burned with fire, and the bush was not consumed" (Exodus 3:2). This glorious presence does not convey a verbal message but instead manifests the sheer miracle of God's power. In the following verses, it is the Lord who speaks with Moses and gives him instruction, taking the role of messenger (that is, one who conveys information) himself. Thus the reference to the angel describes the manifestation of the Lord's glory, the miraculous arm of the Lord, rather than an embodied being or spiritual personage. This pattern of imagery continues in the descriptions of the pillar of fire and cloud by night as the Israelites wander in the wilderness. "And the angel of God, which went before the camp of Israel, removed and went behind them; and the pillar of the cloud went

---

2. "Harden not your heart, as in the provocation, and as in the day of temptation in the wilderness: When your fathers tempted me, proved me, and saw my work. Forty years long was I grieved with this generation, and said, It is a people that do err in their heart, and they have not known my ways: Unto whom I sware in my wrath that they should not enter into my rest" (Psalm 95:8–11).

"Wherefore we labored diligently among our people that we might persuade them to come unto Christ and partake of the goodness of God, that they might enter into his rest, lest by any means he should swear in his wrath they should not enter in, as in the provocation in the days of temptation while the children of Israel were in the wilderness" (Jacob 1:7).

"Wherefore (as the Holy Ghost saith, To day if ye will hear his voice, Harden not your hearts, as in the provocation, in the day of temptation in the wilderness: When your fathers tempted me, proved me, and saw my works forty years. Wherefore I was grieved with that generation, and said, They do alway err in their heart; and they have not known my ways. So I sware in my wrath, They shall not enter into my rest)" (Hebrews 3:7–11).

from before their face, and stood behind them" (Exodus 14:19). Here the angel functions in precisely the same role as the pillar of fire and cloud. The angel *is* the miracle itself. And in the exodus story, these miracles are redemptive, guiding and protecting the Israelites as they escape their enemies, traverse harsh landscapes, and are eventually established in the land of promise. With these points in mind, Alma 12:29–30 might be annotated with new narrative details:

> Therefore he [God] sent angels [his own miraculous power] to converse with [guide, defend] them [Moses and the children of Israel], which caused men to behold of his glory. And they [Moses and the children of Israel] began from that time forth to call on his name; therefore God conversed with men and made known unto them the plan of redemption which had been prepared from the foundation of the world.

Who is the angel, and what is glory in this story? Rather than a specific being or beings, the angel or angels of the exodus are the very manifestation of glory itself, that is, a miraculous divine power. This glory both signals Moses's initiation to his prophetic calling and delivers the children of Israel from danger. As such, this angelic or divine glory prepares the Hebrews for the reception of the law and is instrumental in establishing them as a covenant nation.

With allusions to the Adam and Eve story and the exodus narrative, Alma's description of the angelic commission can be set in both a mythical and historical context. Allusions to the Genesis story (a mythological narrative in its explanation of human origins) invite application to all humanity. The learning process required for God's plan to be enacted is one that rises out of a universal mortal experience. In the Genesis story, the cherubim's glory enacts the laws of life and death. Humanity is now time bound, as the threatening presence of the angel guards Adam and Eve from the tree of life, but this enforced mortality leads to Adam and Eve's active role in calling upon God, conversing with him, and receiving the divine knowledge of the plan of redemption.

But the layered allusions to the exodus narrative remind listeners and readers that a sequence of divine tutelage is repeated over the course of history. In an exodus reading of Alma's narrative, angelic glory precedes the law of Moses, not a universal law, but one that defined a nation or ethnos. This revelation of glory provides temporal redemption, delivering the Israelites from death and physical bondage. The process of learning described here is therefore renewable and cyclical. God reveals his glory to prepare for a holy order of law and commandments.

Alma: Angels and personal conversion

But these allusions to the remote mythical beginnings of the world and to the historical establishment of the Israelite nation are not the only narratives that can be extracted from Alma's sermon. After all, the purpose of Alma's sermon is evangelical: he hopes to prompt in his listeners a personal conversion, and thus the importance of this brief narrative of angels depends not only on its links to biblical tradition but on its relevance to Alma's listeners. Another textual allusion is key here: Alma's own personal conversion narrative. Alma's harrowing encounter with divine glory comes in Mosiah 27: When an angel speaks to him with a voice of thunder, Alma is left racked with guilt and unable to speak or move for three days. He emerges from this state only after calling upon the name of Christ, and from this moment on, he is a devoted disciple. Alma's own experience follows the pattern of learning he describes in Alma 12:29–30. After his dramatic conversion, Alma calls upon the Lord seeking knowledge. Answers to his questions come not in a blaze of glory but as understated but revelatory dialogue with God or his Spirit. He describes this process in Alma 5:46, "Behold, I say unto you: They are made known unto me by the Holy Spirit of God. Behold, I have fasted and prayed many days that I might know these things of myself. And now I do know of myself that they are true, for the Lord God hath made them manifest unto me by his Holy Spirit."

With Alma's personal story in mind, we could annotate Alma 12:29–30 thus:

> Therefore he [God] sent angels to converse with them [Alma and his companions], which caused men [Alma et al.] to behold of his glory [and experience a preview of divine judgment]. And they [Alma] began from that time forth to call on his name; therefore God conversed with men [through his Holy Spirit] and made known unto them the plan of redemption which had been prepared from the foundation of the world.

Who is the angel and what is glory in this story? Alma's angel is a personal messenger, sent by God's grace and the prayers of his father to convince him of the "power and authority of God" (Mosiah 27:14). This angel speaks "with a voice of thunder" (v. 11) and physically incapacitates his listeners. But more importantly in this story, he also prompts in Alma a spiritual recognition of his own guilt. The emphasis of the conversion story of Mosiah 27 (as well as later retellings) on Alma's interior or spiritual experience sets it apart from the Genesis and exodus narratives. While Alma does witness a physical or external divine power during his encounter with the angel, the real power comes with Alma's visionary glimpse of his own final judgment: this internalized and intimately personal vision of the glory of God racks him with horror at his own guilt. But both types of glory (external physical power and internal vision) lead to his eventual conversion in Christ.

Ammonihah: Angels and astonishment

Shifting the context of Alma 12:28–30 from biblical narratives to Alma's own conversion means changing perspective from collective history to personal narrative, from stories of external miracles to one of internalized conversion. But if Alma's pattern of personal conversion is to have relevance to his immediate audience, then we are faced with a potential problem. How are Alma's listeners to follow this pattern of learning without an angel to reveal divine glory to them? If the angelic commission is necessary to the human learning process, then where are the angels in the context of the conversions that take place during Alma's mission to Ammonihah? The frame narrative of Alma's sermon offers possible answers to this question. Immediately before the dialogue exchange between Antionah and Alma, the narrator (probably Mormon) records, "Now . . . when Alma had made an end of speaking these words, the people began to be more astonished" (Alma 12:19). If we trace the use of this word *astonished* in scripture, it becomes clear that this reaction goes beyond mere surprise. Rather, *astonishment* is a term used to convey recognition of God's power, the fear and trembling prompted by miraculous events. In the Old Testament, *astonishment* is often used in contexts of divine punishments or the just consequences of transgression, as in Deuteronomy 28:28, when Moses pronounces a curse on lawbreakers: "The Lord shall smite thee with madness, and blindness, and astonishment of heart." The use of this word shifts in the New Testament toward a context of preaching and conversation. Unaccompanied by any physical miracle, Jesus's doctrine alone prompts astonishment in his listeners (see Matthew 22:33 and Mark 1:22). Again, in these instances, astonishment indicates a response that goes beyond surprise; it signals a recognition of Jesus's authority, as in Luke 4:32: "And they were astonished at his doctrine: for his word was with power." Similar descriptions of astonishment at the words of a speaker can be seen in the Book of Mormon, and these contexts likewise convey an implication of the miraculous power of God: When Sherem admits his deception and acknowledges God's power, his listeners are so "astonished" that they are "overcome" and fall "to the earth" (Jacob 7:21). The priests of Noah listen to the words of Abinadi "to their astonishment," as he withstands the questions of the priests and "confound[s] them in all their words" (Mosiah 12:19). But most relevant to this discussion, Alma's own conversion is prompted by astonishment. When the angel speaks in a voice of thunder that shakes the earth, "so great was their astonishment that they fell to the earth" (Mosiah 27:12). In fact, the word's etymology can be traced to the Latin *extonare* or "out-thunder." To be astonished is to be thunderstruck, as Alma's conversion experience confirms. Alma and his friends have no choice but to recognize God's divine power and glory.

Now, years after this conversion, Alma meets the same angel, receiving from him a direct commission to preach repentance (Alma 8:14–17). With Mormon's tag-word *astonished*, readers are alerted to the narrative parallel. In the encounters that follow, Alma takes on the characteristics of his own guardian angel as he and Amulek demonstrate the same power to set their listeners at profound unease. His words in Alma 12 show clear parallels to his own conversion. Consider his warning to the unrepentant people of Ammonihah: "We would fain be glad if we could command the rocks and the mountains to fall upon us, to hide us from his presence" (Alma 12:14). This parallels the description of his own conversion in Alma 36:15, "O, thought I, that I could be banished and become extinct, both soul and body, that I might not be brought to stand in the presence of my God to be judged of my deeds." This is followed with a declaration of Christ's power to save "every man that believeth on his name" (Alma 12:15), again echoing Alma's own recognition of Christ's saving power at the moment of his own conversion. Alma's angelic visitor prompted a harrowing individual conversion experience, and his later deputized angelic power in Ammonihah has a similarly harrowing effect. The astonished response of his hearers demonstrates their recognition of God's power.

An annotated version of Alma 12:29–30 to reflect the learning process of the Ammonihahites themselves reads thus:

> Therefore he [God, through his angel] sent angels [Alma himself] to converse with them [the Ammonihahites], which caused men to behold of his glory [be astonished at the power of God]. And they began from that time forth to call on his name; therefore God conversed with men and made known unto them the plan of redemption which had been prepared from the foundation of the world. And this he made known unto them according to their faith and repentance and their holy works.

Only some of Alma's listeners—Amulek, Zeezrom, and others—eventually call upon God and engage in the learning process of faith, repentance, and holy works. Others resist with outright violence against God's word.

Who is the angel? For the Ammonihahites, the angel is Alma, a commissioned messenger sent to them by God. What is glory? Instead of externalized miracles or physical displays of divine power, the people of Ammonihah experience internalized astonishment.

Reading Alma's sequence of glory and order within a context contemporary to Alma himself and the people of Ammonihah broadens the potential application of the angelic commission. Alma's deputized but nonetheless angelic confrontation with the people of Ammonihah shows that the revelation of the glory of God occurs by various means. This is a question not just of God's establishing covenant nations or setting the bounds for the human race as a whole. Rather, God's sequence of instruction serves the individual at any moment in time. This spiritual revelation of glory prompts personal conversions and prepares individuals to understand the plan of redemption.

Angels and a theology of glory

To summarize, Alma's short narrative of only three verses posits the angelic manifestation of God's glory as a necessary forerunner to the work of understanding and enacting the plan of redemption. The sermon in which this short narrative is embedded is rich with intertextual references to biblical tradition and allusions to Alma's own personal history—an intertextuality that suggests (at least) four distinct narrative contexts for this three-verse sequence. The Genesis narrative gives foundational and collective significance to the angelic commission of glory, establishing the boundaries of life and death for all humanity. Chief among its aftereffects is the possibility of redemption. Alma's allusions to the exodus story demonstrate a repetition of this angelic commission throughout temporal history. Within this context, the revelation of miraculous power establishes covenant nations and opens new dispensations in time. The third story, considered an allusion to Alma's own conversion, presents readers with a personalized learning process. In this context, Alma acknowledges God's glorious power as both external and internal experience. Alma's astonishment at the appearance of the angel is demonstrated not only by his physical weakness, but also by his intense soul-searching and ultimate conversion. Finally, Mormon's descriptions of the people of Ammonihah also place them within this sequence of learning, as they feel astonishment at the angelic words of Alma and recognize spiritual truth. Alma's narratives range from the macrocosmic story of humanity itself to the intensely personal processes of individual conversion.

These narratives demonstrate how God's urgency to make the plan of redemption known to the children of men is answered with a two-part sequence. Stated simply, God first reveals his power or glory. Second comes the giving of the law, commandments that require faith and repentance. In these narratives, glory is given chronological priority, happening without human instigation or the practice of holy works. If we give this glory theological definition, it seems possible to identify it with the concept of grace. That is, glory can be defined as a miraculous power that works independently of merits of humanity, preceding faith and repentance. Alma insists upon the unasked-for grace of his own angelic encounter: "Now behold, I say unto you: If I had not been born of God, I should not have known these things. But God has by the mouth of his holy angel made these things known unto me, not of any worthiness of myself" (Alma 36:5).

What gives some pause is the distinctly frightening quality of these astonishing moments. Adam and Eve's expulsion from the Garden of Eden or Alma's prostration at the encounter with the angel do not seem like the tender mercies that the concept of grace usually conveys. However, Alma's narrative asserts their legitimate place in the merciful plan of redemption. The grace of angelic glory is not tender or soothing but disruptive, even violent. If the giving of the law can be described as ordered and instructive, the manifestation of glory is revelatory but harrowing, even (as in Alma's conversion) a preview of a final judgment. Nonetheless, it moves humanity forward and initiates their redemption.

While giving narrative context to these verses may clarify some questions, it also complicates others. Alma presents these two modes of communication in chronological sequence, but their occurrence in multiple periods of history and on both collective and individual levels necessarily blurs the linear sequence of his language. This overlay of multiple narratives creates a dynamic and cyclical interaction out of what is framed in linear terms. Why cite the revelation of glory first? Might it be useful to look beyond a chronological sequence and toward a sequence of logical priority with glory's juxtaposition with ordered law and holy works? Can we see the revelation of glory as coming first in importance rather than in time? Perhaps we can say that God's plan of redemption requires a foundation of strength, power, and glory upon which good works can build. This unasked-for and unmerited glory must precede human works of faith and repentance, and the plan of redemption can only be enacted with an initial manifestation of miraculous power. Thus while Alma's continued sermon describes a structured holy order, with all the human exchange that that entails and with earthly learning processes blended with divine tutelage, one reality is necessary: the glory and grace of God. If we apply this logical priority to Alma's sequence of making known the plan of redemption, then what matters here is not angels as divine beings but the glory that they reveal. And in our process of learning, that glory is crucial. Without the priority of miraculous grace, law and order cannot take effect. Humanity may start with blind obedience to commandments, but in the sequence of God's plan of redemption, the miracle of grace always comes first. It is first because it is also eternal.

In this final theological narrative, who are the angels and what is the glory? In Alma's sermon on the holy order of the priesthood following this initial sequence in Alma 12:29, angels are absent. Instead, Alma focuses on an explanation of commandments, holy works, and the holy order of priesthood. But I would assert that the glory that angels are commissioned to reveal remains embedded in the process of learning that Alma sets forth. In Alma's final passage on Melchizedek, he describes the organization of the priesthood as the ultimate context for divine learning and the entry point into the rest of the Lord. Alma 13:8 reads, "Now they were ordained after this manner: being called with a holy calling and ordained with a holy ordinance and taking upon them the high priesthood of the holy order—which calling and ordinance and high priesthood is without beginning or end." The repetition of "holy" in this verse is key: holy calling, holy ordinance, holy order. This holiness echoes the call of the seraphim in Isaiah 6:1–3: "I saw also the Lord sitting upon a throne, high and lifted up, and his train filled the temple. Above it stood the seraphims. . . . And one cried unto another, and said, Holy, holy, holy, is the Lord of hosts: the whole earth is full of his glory." The call of the seraphim is identical to the angelic commission detailed in the above four narratives. As these angels reveal the glory of God, this glory is not one in a series of isolated manifestations. It fills the earth.

Here the distinction between glory and the ordered holy works of faith and repentance is blurred. The holy order described by Alma is a reinstitution of the miracle of God's power, a typology of his grace and glory. This grace and glory of God, which work independently of any human will, eventually fill the lives of those who are truly converted. Humanity's holy works of peace and repentance, the hallmark of the priesthood of Alma 13, are therefore works of grace as well. The divine urgency to make the plan of redemption known to humanity is always already answered by the divine grace of God's glory. It becomes humanity's privilege to recognize and take part in the glory infused throughout creation. Within the holy order of God, angels are among us, and glory is continually made manifest.

The Heart in Alma 12 and 13

Robert A. Rees

THE HEART IS ONE OF THE MOST POTENT and prevalent symbols in human culture and is central to the traditions and sacred texts of the world's major religions. The word *heart* or *hearts* appears more than a thousand times in the Bible and figures prominently in the Qur'an, the Upanishads, the Tao Te Ching, and other sacred texts, including the Book of Mormon, where it appears nearly seven hundred times between 1 Nephi and Moroni. This paper examines the symbolism of the heart in Alma 12:19–13:20. The discussion includes insights from ancient spiritual traditions as well as new scientific discoveries about the heart in psychology, physiology, and neurocardiology.

The heart was seen anciently as the locus of the mind and the soul and, in some traditions, even of being itself. The ancients understood truths and mysteries about the heart that are being validated by modern science. According to Rollin McCraty and Robert Rees, "Scientific research has established the existence of complex, highly sophisticated neural pathways that connect the human heart and brain, confirming that the activity of the heart directly influences the activity of higher brain centers involved in perceptual and cognitive processing and in the creation of emotional experience."[1] Beyond this, "The heart's

1. Rollin McCraty and Robert A. Rees, "New Perspectives on the Role of the Heart in Positive Emotions, Intuition, and Social Coherence," in *Handbook of Positive*

intrinsic nervous system is a sophisticated information-encoding and processing center that operates independently of the brain."[2]

The association of volition, cognition, and memory with the heart was central to the consciousness of the Israelites. As Gail Godwin notes, "For the ancient Hebrews, heart, *lev*, meant the seat of wisdom and understanding, the inner personality, the whole gamut of emotional life, as well as the collective mind, or mind-set, of the people: the mental as well as the fleshly heart."[3] According to Mircea Eliade, for the Hebrews "the heart is the locus not only of the whole psychological and intellectual life but also of moral life."[4] R. C. Dentan observes, "Because of its concrete character, the Hebrew language can hardly express the idea 'to think' except by the phrase 'to say in the heart.'"[5] Many Old Testament scriptures express this idea. For example, in Proverbs we read, "Apply thine heart to understanding" (2:2) and "As he thinketh in his heart, so is he" (23:7). Various scriptures suggest that just as God wrote the Ten Commandments on stone tablets, so he writes his word on people's hearts (e.g., Jeremiah 31:33, a scripture Paul quotes in Hebrews 8:10). Alma 12:7 speaks of "the thoughts and intents" of the heart, and later in Alma we read: "And there was no unequality among them, for the Lord did pour out his Spirit on all the face of the land for to prepare the minds of the children of men, or to prepare their hearts to receive the word which should be taught among them at the time of his coming, that they might not be hardened against the word,

---

Psychology, 3rd ed., ed. C. R. Snyder, Shane J. Lopez, Lisa M. Edwards, and Susana C. Marques (Oxford: Oxford University Press, 2017).

2. Rollin McCraty and Robert A. Rees, "The Heart-Brain Connection," in *The Encyclopedia of Positive Psychology* (Oxford: Wiley-Blackwell, 2009), 472; for additional insights on the heart-brain connection, see Rollin McCraty, Mike Atkinson, et al., *The Coherent Heart: Heart–Brain Interactions, Psychophysiological Coherence, and the Emergence of System-Wide Order* (Boulder Creek, CA: The Institute of HeartMath, 2006).

3. Gail Godwin, *Heart: A Personal Journey through Its Myths and Meanings* (New York: William Morrow, 2001), 35.

4. Mircea Eliade, ed., *The Encyclopedia of Religion* (New York: Macmillan, 1987), 234.

5. R. C. Dentan, *Preface to Old Testament Theology* (1962), 550, as cited in Glen H. Elder Jr., *The Body, An Encyclopedia of Archetypical Symbolism*, vol. 2 (Boston: Shambhala, 1996), 288.

that they might not be unbelieving and go on to destruction, but that they might receive the word with joy" (Alma 16:16–17)[6]—or in other words that they might feel God's love in their hearts, what Rumi called "the deep ear inside the chest."[7]

Thus, this rich, deep, and multifaceted understanding of the heart was carried by the people of Lehi as they crossed the Arabian Desert and the great ocean to reach their new home in the promised land. It was embedded not only in the brass plates but also in their hearts and minds.

Reference to the heart in the Book of Mormon, and specifically in these chapters in Alma, is rooted in the rich cultures and languages of ancient Near Eastern peoples. There are sixteen references to the heart in Alma 12 and 13, more than in any other two contiguous chapters in the Book of Mormon. Of the sixteen references, twelve include the figure of a hardened heart, an image that is found some eighty-four times among the multiple references to heart in the Book of Mormon. "Hardness of heart" is also a figure found in the Bible, but far less frequently than in the history of the Lehites. Of the 1,075 mentions of the heart in the Old and New Testaments, only nine refer to a hardened heart, and all nine are in scriptural texts that would have been found on the brass plates and therefore represent a possible source for the writers of the Book of Mormon.

The idea of a hard or hardened heart among the people of the Book of Mormon is introduced in the second chapter of 1 Nephi, where Nephi tells us, "Having great desires to know of the mysteries of God, . . . I cried unto the Lord. And behold, he did visit me and did soften my heart" (1 Nephi 2:16). That is, for all his greatness, Nephi did not begin with a softened heart but prayed for one. Thus, the story of these New World peoples begins with a hard heart that becomes softened. Two verses later we meet Nephi's brothers, Laman and Lemuel, who, Nephi tells us, "would not hearken unto my words . . . because of the hardness of their hearts" (v. 18). These brothers soften their hearts periodically

6. Herein, I use Royal Skousen's edition of the Book of Mormon.

7. Rumi, "Listening," in *The Glance: Songs of Soul Meeting*, trans. Coleman Barks (New York: Penguin Compass, 1999), n.p.

but always, it seems, reluctantly and temporarily as they continue to resist the importunings and pleadings of their father, younger brother, other members of the clan, and even angels.

The nature and dimensions of a hardened heart are summarized in the following:

> The heart, in effect, is the whole person in all of his or her distinctive human activity as a thinking, planning, willing, feeling, worshiping, and socially interacting being. And, of course, when the person is not living according to God's will, it is the heart that is described as darkened, rebellious, callous, unfeeling, or idolatrous. It is within the heart that God works; hence the human heart may be tender and soft or as hard as stone (Ezekiel 11:19). It is in this context that hardening or hardness of the heart must be understood. The heart represents the total response of a person to life around him or her and to the religious and moral demands of God. Hardness of heart thus describes a negative condition in which the person ignores, spurns, or rejects the gracious offer of God to be a part of his or her life.[8]

The drama that unfolds in the Book of Mormon can be seen as an archetypal conflict between those who strive to have softened (i.e., humble, receptive, teachable, and, ultimately, loving) hearts and those who choose to keep hard (i.e., resistant, recalcitrant, callous, and, ultimately, unloving) hearts. The last image we get of the heart in the Book of Mormon is in the next to last chapter of Moroni, where we are told the people whom Mormon is calling to repentance "harden their hearts against it [i.e., the word of God]." Such hardness means that "they have no fear of death. And they have lost their love one towards another; and they thirst after blood and revenge continually" (Moroni 9:4–5), or, as Mormon says just a few verses later, they are "without

---

8. Walter A. Elwell, "Hardening, Hardness of Heart," in *Baker's Evangelical Dictionary of Biblical Theology*, http://classic.studylight.org/dic/bed/view.cgi?number=T322.

civilization" (v. 11), an amazingly damning condemnation. Thus, the Book of Mormon begins with one softened heart (Nephi's) and ends with an entire nation possessed of adamantly hardened hearts. That seems to summarize the history of these New World peoples as succinctly as one could imagine.

In the book of Alma we have another Nephite whose heart is softened. Alma the Younger had been among those who "did not believe the tradition of their fathers . . . concerning the resurrection of the dead, neither did they believe concerning the coming of Christ," with the result that "their hearts were hardened" (Mosiah 26:1–3). When Alma came of age "he became a very wicked and an idolatrous man . . . [who] led many of the people to do after the manner of his iniquities, . . . stealing away the hearts of the people" (Mosiah 27:8–9). When an angel appears to Alma and his companions and rebukes them for their wickedness, out of "the darkest abyss" of his guilt and shame, Alma beholds "the marvelous light of God" (Mosiah 27:29) and experiences a mighty change of heart, just as his father had earlier upon hearing the words of Abinadi. Having had his own heart softened, Alma seeks to soften the hearts of others, which leads him to renounce his role as chief judge and preach the gospel "throughout the land" of Zarahemla (headnote Alma 5). After teaching the citizens of the city of Zarahemla, Alma asks, "Have ye spiritually been born of God? Have ye received his image in your own countenances? Have ye experienced this mighty change in your hearts?" (Alma 5:14) Those questions, directly or indirectly, are the subject of the sermons of Alma and his companions throughout their missionary journeys and ultimately of all the prophets who preach and teach among the Nephites and Lamanites.

Although Alma's preaching has a positive impact on some of his hearers, not everyone in Zarahemla experiences a profound change of heart. Some continue to be "puffed up in the pride of [their] hearts," while others set their "hearts upon the vain things of the world [and] upon [their] riches" (Alma 5:53).

After leaving Zarahemla, Alma preaches in succession in Gideon, Melek, and Ammonihah where, we are told, "Satan had got great hold upon the hearts of the people" (Alma 8:9). Alma prays mightily that

God will pour out his spirit upon the Ammonihahites. "Nevertheless," we are told, "they hardened their hearts" (v. 11), and many remained "a hard-hearted and a stiffnecked people" (Alma 9:5). Their hearts have not just been hardened but "grossly hardened" (v. 30).

Hoping to persuade them to soften their hearts, Alma's missionary companion, Amulek, confesses that, like them, he once had a hardened and wicked heart (Alma 10:6), but, like his friend Alma, his heart was changed when an angel appeared to him. The narrative then turns to one Zeezrom who tries to manipulate and, ultimately, destroy Amulek by bribery and trickery, but Amulek discerns his intent—"thou had it in thy heart . . . that thou mightest have cause to destroy me" (Alma 11:25). Caught in his deception and realizing that he is about to be trapped in "a snare of the adversary" (Alma 12:6), Zeezrom is convinced that Alma and Amulek "knew the thoughts and intents of his heart" (v. 7). This is an interesting construction—the idea of reading hearts rather than minds, but it is in accord with other scriptures that locate thoughts in the heart.

All this is prelude to what transpires in Alma 12–13 where, as pointed out above, there are a dozen references within a short space to the trope of hardening one's heart. These include such expressions as "he that will harden his heart," "he that will not harden his heart" (Alma 12:10); and "if our hearts have been hardened—yea, if we have hardened our hearts against the word" (v. 13). Alma quotes God himself as pleading with his children not to harden their hearts: "But God did call upon men in the name of his Son, . . . saying: If ye will repent and harden not your hearts, then will I have mercy upon you through mine Only Begotten Son. Therefore whosoever repenteth and hardeneth not his heart, he shall have claim on mercy. . . . And whosoever will harden his heart and will do iniquity, behold, I swear in my wrath that they shall not enter into my rest" (vv. 33–35). Having God speak these warning words about hardening one's heart gives more force to Alma's speaking to them right after, especially when he identifies himself with his hard-hearted listeners: "And now my brethren, seeing we know these things and they are true, let *us* repent and harden not *our* hearts" (v. 37). One could argue that it takes a softened heart to identify and empathize with a hardened heart. In essence, this is what Jesus does and what he asks us to do.

What does it mean to harden one's heart? According to Webster's 1828 dictionary, *hardness* means "to make obstinate, unyielding or refractory; to confirm in wickedness, opposition or enmity; to make insensible or unfeeling."[9] Within the context of these chapters, it clearly means to deliberately resist the whisperings and entreaties of the Spirit, to willfully ignore and reject the messages of angels and prophets, to be proud and unteachable, to shut down the tender feelings of the heart, to spurn the gift of mercy offered through Jesus Christ, and to attempt to persuade others to harden their hearts. It is to prefer darkness over light, sin over righteousness and, ultimately, death over life.

Interestingly, having an open heart and knowing truth are closely linked in these scriptures. In responding to Antionah's disingenuous question about the fall, Alma informs him that God "saw that it was expedient that man should know concerning the things whereof he had appointed unto them. Therefore he sent angels to converse with them" (Alma 12:28–29). When men "began from that time forth to call on his name, . . . God conversed with men and made known unto them the plan of redemption" (v. 30). It is clear that those who have closed, calloused, or hardened hearts cannot know the things of God or, having once known them, reject that knowledge. Conversely, those with open and softened hearts not only seek but thirst for knowledge. As Godwin states, "The intelligence of the heart is a special kind of imaginative intelligence which combines knowing and loving in a single function. It is a way of seeing with the heart."[10]

Remembering is related to both knowing and having a receptive or softened heart. It is clear from the various discourses about faith and knowledge that take place in the book of Alma that those who have hardened hearts fail to remember the tender mercies of the Lord. One archaic meaning of to "re-member" is "to pass through the heart

---

9. *American Dictionary of the English Language*, online ed., s.v. "hardness," http://webstersdictionary1828.com/Dictionary/hardness.

10. Godwin, *Heart: A Personal Journey*, 89.

again." Thus, Alma asks the people of Zarahemla who, following their conversion, had "set their hearts upon riches and upon the vain things of the world" (Alma 4:8), "Have you sufficiently retained *in remembrance* the captivity of your fathers? Yea, and have you sufficiently retained *in remembrance* his mercy and long-suffering towards them? And moreover, have ye sufficiently retained *in remembrance* that he has delivered their souls from hell?" (5:6). In other words, he is asking, "Have you sufficiently allowed the personal and cultural memory of your people's bondage to pass through your hearts again? Have you sufficiently held in your hearts a memory of the mercy God showed in delivering them from their captors? Have you allowed the realization of their being free from the pains of hell to penetrate your hearts as in the past?" He follows these challenging questions with a simple declaration, "Behold, he [God] changed their hearts" (v. 7)—with the implication that God stands ready to change theirs as well. Similarly, he says to the people of Ammonihah, "I would that *ye should remember* that the Lord God ordained priests after his holy order, which was after the order of his Son, to teach these things unto the people" (Alma 13:1). It is the heart that feels and that remembers those feelings—or that chooses not to remember and feel.

When God created his mortal children in his image, he created them with hearts like his: hearts that beat, that know and feel, hearts that think and remember, hearts that can feel joy and sorrow, and hearts that can be broken and healed. It is with love that God made us in his image, but it was with a special love that he created us with hearts that feel as his heart feels and love as his heart loves, and this, therefore, gives us the potential to share in his glory and holiness.

Scientists have only recently begun to discover the wonders of the heart—or to discover what prophets, priests, and poets have always known about this mysterious organ at the center of our bodies and being. We now know that the heart has thousands of neurons like the neurons in our brains and, further, that the heart and brain are in constant, dynamic correspondence with one another. We know that a person's heart starts beating before his/her brain is fully formed, suggesting that it has a primary role in initiating human life. We can remain alive once the brain dies, but when the heart stops beating, mortal life ends.

In actuality, "The heart's electrical field is about 60 times greater in amplitude than that generated by the brain, and the magnetic field produced by the heart is more than 5,000 times greater in strength than that produced by the brain."[11] Scientists now postulate that with its own independent nervous system, the heart possesses some kind of cognitive and memory capacity, what neurocardiologists refer to as "the little brain in the heart."[12] Beyond this, the heart seems to have an amazing intuitive capacity that allows it to perceive "information normally outside the range of conscious awareness" and to "respond to an emotionally arousing stimulus seconds before it is actually experienced."[13] These heart-centered precognitive, cognitive, memorial, and intuitional capabilities seem designed by God to communicate his knowledge and love via the heart to our entire systems and to enable us to communicate with him in like manner. In other words, God seems to be trying to reach us—to awaken our hearts, minds, bodies, and souls to the good news of the gospel and to persuade us in multiple ways and by multiple channels to repent and turn to him. As he said to Zachariah, "Therefore say thou unto them, Thus saith the Lord of hosts; Turn ye unto me, . . . and I will turn unto you" (Zachariah 1:3). Turning our hearts to God and turning them to others is possible only when our hearts are softened.

In chapters 12 and 13, Alma calls his brothers and sisters to a life of holiness by teaching them about the plan of redemption, by inviting them to soften and experience a "mighty change" in their hearts, and by persuading them that their eternal happiness, entering into the rest of the Lord, depends on turning their hearts to God.

---

11. McCraty and Rees, "Heart-Brain Connection," 472.

12. Rollin McCraty, Mike Atkinson, and Raymond Trevor Bradley, "Electrophysiological Evidence of Intuition: Part 1. The Surprising Role of the Heart," *Journal of Alternative and Complementary Medicine* 10/1 (June 2004): 133–43. See also parts 2 and 3 in the same journal.

13. McCraty and Rees, "Heart-Brain Connection."

Behind us in this Chapel of the Great Commission[14] hangs a large wooden cross. It is a symbol of a broken heart but also represents a heart that is compassionate, forgiving, merciful, healing, redeeming, and, especially, loving. Christ calls us to break our hearts upon this broken tree and to offer them to him as a sacrifice, but as with all sacrifices he makes a promise: "And ye shall offer for a sacrifice unto me a broken heart and a contrite spirit. And whoso cometh unto me with a broken heart and a contrite spirit, him will I baptize with fire and with the Holy Ghost" (3 Nephi 9:20).

Alma concludes his sermon to the Ammonihahites by speaking about his own heart—"I wish from the inmost part of my heart . . . that ye would hearken unto my words and cast off your sins and not procrastinate the day of your repentance, . . . and thus be led by the Holy Spirit, becoming humble, meek, submissive, patient, full of love and all long-suffering" (Alma 13:27–28). In other words, God invites us, his children, to soften our hearts so that we might learn the lesson he is always hoping we will learn—to know and love ourselves, to love others, and to love his Son and him—*by heart*. It is interesting that when Jesus commanded us to love God completely, he put the heart first: "Thou shalt love the Lord thy God with all thy heart, and with all thy soul, and with all thy mind" (Matthew 22:37), or, as God said to Abraham, "Walk in my presence! And be wholehearted" (Genesis 17:1, Everett Fox translation).

---

14. The 2016 Mormon Theology Seminar Conference was held at the Pacific School of Religion, Chapel of the Great Commission, in Berkeley, California.

Obtaining Divine Mercy

Sheila Taylor

In Alma 12, God's mercy is connected to the plan of redemption and contrasted to God's wrath, which is kindled against the wicked. What is at stake here is God's rest, which is promised to those who obtain his mercy and denied to those who have provoked his wrath. In this paper, I would like to first consider the context of Alma's remarks on these subjects, then ask the question of what is necessary to obtain mercy—in other words, examine the role of human agency in the plan of redemption—and finally briefly consider the role of wrath in all this.

Alma's sermon in the second half of Alma 12 is sparked by the questions of a man named Antionah, a chief ruler of the people of Ammonihah. These people are in a later chapter described as a "hard-hearted and a stiffnecked" people, who "were of the profession of Nehor and did not believe in the repentance of their sins" (Alma 15:15). Nehor taught that priests should be supported by the labor of the people and that there was no reason to fear condemnation, as all humankind would be saved (Alma 1:3–4). While in this text Alma initially discusses the specific subject raised by Antionah, his continued comments indicate a concern with Nehorite teachings more generally.

The question that Antionah poses to Alma has to do with the resurrection of the dead and the notion that humans will at that point be changed from mortality to immortality. He points out that God placed cherubim and a flaming sword to protect the tree of life precisely so that Adam and Eve would be unable to partake of that fruit and live forever. Alma responds not with a robust defense of the doctrine of resurrection, which one might expect, but with an explanation of why the tree of life had to be guarded: if Adam and Eve could have taken the fruit, it would have made God a liar, for God told them they would die from eating the forbidden fruit; also, it would have made the first couple "forever miserable" (Alma 12:26) because they would have been trapped in a state of sin, with no chance for repentance.

This is not to say that Alma ignores the resurrection, which he says is contingent on the plan of redemption. But he is more concerned with the issue of judgment and this life as a "probationary state" in which we "prepare to meet God" (Alma 12:24). He goes on to discuss God's communicating these things to humans, first by sending angels and then through conversing with them directly. God also gives commandments, first in Eden and then after. Those who violate the latter, those commandments given after the fall, are under penalty of the second death, "an everlasting death as to things pertaining unto righteousness" (v. 32). The plan of redemption does not save those in this situation because "the works of justice could not be destroyed" (v. 32).

It is at this point that we get the first explicit mention of mercy in this section of Alma's sermon. God calls on humankind, in the name of the Son, and says, "If ye will repent and harden not your hearts, then will I have mercy upon you through mine Only Begotten Son" (Alma 12:33). One can see God's mercy at work in much of what has been related up until now: in the granting of a temporal state in which repentance is possible, for example, and in reaching out to humans to communicate the plan of redemption. But the term only shows up explicitly following a discussion of the possibility of spiritual death and the works of justice.

While it is striking that the word *mercy* appears only after justice has come on the scene, Alma does not here develop a theology of justice and mercy. Rather, he goes on to talk about wrath: the opposite of mercy in these verses is not justice but wrath. Those who repent and do not harden their hearts "have claim on mercy" through the Son (Alma 12:34). By contrast, those who harden their hearts will find that their iniquity provokes God into sending his wrath. The rest of the Lord is promised to the penitent, and those who do iniquity are warned that they will not enter into it. As in his earlier comments about life as a probationary state, Alma emphasizes the significance of the choices humans make during mortality. This account may have wandered a bit from Antionah's initial question about resurrection, but it makes sense as a refutation of Nehorite theology generally, given Alma's emphasis on repentance and his teaching that redemption is not something automatic for all but is contingent on human behavior.

This raises a crucial question: what exactly is required of humans for salvation? For the Nehorites, nothing. By contrast, this section of Alma 12 refers to three sets of human actions. First of all, faith, repentance, and holy works are somehow involved in God's making known the plan of redemption. Second, humans—who after the fall can choose good from evil—are commanded not to choose evil. And third—and, I will argue, most crucially—those who repent and harden not their hearts are said to have claim on mercy.

As mentioned earlier, Alma explains that God wishes to communicate with humans about their situation, and he therefore sends angels—a move that sparks human action, namely the action of calling on God. God then makes known the plan of redemption to humans, "according to their faith and repentance and their holy works" (Alma 12:30). One way to read this passage is as saying that God only shares knowledge of redemption with those who are righteous. But this seems unlikely, particularly since Alma is preaching these things to the not-so-righteous people of Ammonihah. Another possibility is that God only *directly* gives this knowledge to those who have demonstrated faith, repentance, and holy works—and those who have it then have the obligation to share it with others. This would go well with the model of priests described in Alma 13, where priests are described as having "exceeding faith and good works" (v. 3), as having chosen to repent (v. 10), and as having the responsibility to teach others (v. 6). One other possible way to think about this is as describing not intellectual knowledge but experiential. Humans come to know the plan as they participate in it; there is a sense of "knowing" that you can have only through living something.

What is the role of commandments in the plan of redemption? Alma here brings up commandments with reference to Adam and

Eve, who are given initial commandments, one of which they transgress. They are subsequently given a second set of commandments, instructing them not to do evil. A crucial question is whether Adam and Eve actually have the ability to follow these commandments. Alma explains that as a result of the fall, our first parents became "as Gods, knowing good from evil," and that they were in a state where they could "act according to their wills and pleasures, whether to do evil or to do good" (Alma 12:31). On the face of it, this sounds like they are presented with good and evil as equal possibilities and with a will that can opt for either one. But I would like to raise some questions about that interpretation.

When Latter-day Saints talk about Adam and Eve's ability to choose, we often do so in a somewhat Pelagian fashion. Pelagius was a fifth-century thinker whose dispute about the nature of freedom with the great theologian Augustine continues to resonate in theological thinking today.[1] In the Pelagian view, humans exist in a kind of morally neutral condition in which they are equally able to choose good or evil. Freedom refers to the ability to opt for one or the other of these choices. Significantly, in a Pelagian understanding, the will itself cannot be contaminated or corrupted by sin; it is merely that which chooses sin (or chooses otherwise). Its freedom is constituted by this indifference; it is because of its lack of inclination toward any particular course of action that it can be considered truly free. For Pelagius, perfection—always choosing the good—is therefore a theoretical possibility.

The Pelagian view may be appealing, but it is not without its weaknesses. The notion that we can independently and autonomously choose good frequently turns out to be a terrible burden, as we continually fail to live up to our ideals. One might well ask, If we have this kind of freedom, why do we all end up in the same place, ensnared in sin? In addition, this view does not reflect the actual experience of

1. The Pelagian-Augustinian debate has been extensively discussed in the history of Christian theology. For those looking for a basic introduction to the issues at stake, useful overviews can be found in the chapters dealing with Augustine in Roger Haight's *The Experience of Language of Grace* (New York: Paulist Press, 1979), and in Stephen J. Duffy's *The Dynamics of Grace: Perspectives in Theological Anthropology* (Collegeville, MN: The Liturgical Press, 1993).

choosing, as we do not make decisions in some neutral setting carefully insulated from the world. And, troublingly, if we talk about sin as one of the choices available to a neutral will, sin becomes an expression of freedom, rather than something that diminishes it.

For an alternative view, we can turn to Augustine, who emphasized the power of original sin and, in particular, its effects on human freedom. For Augustine, the will is never neutral; it is always inclined in some direction. It does not exist in some isolated, detached sphere from which it surveys good and evil and then makes a choice between them. Rather, it is inherently connected to desire, as our actions are always motivated by some belief about what is good and an inclination in that direction. For Augustine, then, sin is not just outside the will, a choice presented to it—rather, it actually infects it, inclining it toward evil. We are free in a fallen state in that we can follow our desires. But our desire is to sin, which means we are not free to choose the good. Sin is sinful not because we could have chosen differently (as in the Pelagian scheme), but because it opposes God. From this perspective, the freedom described by the Pelagians is not simply an inaccurate understanding of the human situation; it is actually itself a sinful state of being, because it is neutral toward God, rather than desiring God.[2]

Let us return to Alma's observation about Adam and Eve. As mentioned earlier, he says that Adam and Eve were in a state to "act according to their wills and pleasures, whether to do evil or to do good" (Alma 12:31). Significantly, in bringing up pleasure in this context, he incorporates desire as an aspect of the freedom to act, which is an Augustinian move to make. At the very least, I see no reason to automatically assume a Pelagian sort of freedom here, in which humans have a neutral will and equal opportunities to choose good or evil. Alma's description does not preclude the possibility that the will is oriented in a particular direction. Is there reason to think that this could in fact be the case? Alma says that because of the transgression of our first parents, "all mankind became a lost and a fallen people"

---

2. For a helpful discussion of these dynamics, see Alistair McFadyen, *Bound to Sin: Abuse, Holocaust, and the Christian Doctrine of Sin* (Cambridge: Cambridge University Press, 2000), 185–87.

(v. 22). His views on this also appear in his later discourse to his son Corianton, where he describes fallen humans as "*carnal*, *sensual*, and *devilish* by nature" (Alma 42:10).[3] None of this sounds like a neutral state. In fact, being neutral toward God does not seem to be an option in the scriptures. And if our wills have been corrupted, our ability to follow the commandments, to choose the good, is hindered.

What does that mean for the potential for redemption? At this point it is important to note that obedience to commandments is not actually here described as salvific. Strikingly, in these verses in Alma 12, Alma mentions penalty but no reward. In other words, God does not say, keep these commandments to enter into my rest—instead, he simply warns that those who transgress will suffer "an everlasting death as to things pertaining unto righteousness" (Alma 12:32). This one-sidedness may indicate something about the fallenness of the human situation. It is also striking that these commandments are said to be given *after* the plan of redemption—suggesting the priority of the former. The commandments are not laid from the foundation of the world; they do not show up until after the fall. The plan of redemption is more basic to God's purposes. And the plan of redemption addresses the dilemma of the human situation—specifically, the problem of sin—in a way that the commandments do not, as here the commandments just set up humans to be punished for falling short.[4]

In the next verse, Alma 12:33, we finally learn exactly what the plan of redemption is. God calls on humans in the name of the Son, telling them that if they will repent and not harden their hearts, he will have

---

3. This echoes the words of Abinadi, who also describes humans as carnal, sensual, and devilish and says that the devil has power over them (Mosiah 16:3). Such language is also found in the Book of Moses (5:13; 6:49). A similar viewpoint can be found in the words of King Benjamin, who stated that the "the natural man is an enemy to God and has been from the fall of Adam" (Mosiah 3:19).

4. Why does God give commandments, if fallen humans cannot keep them, and they in and of themselves do not have the power to save? One possibility is that they lead to the knowledge of sin—which is what Paul says the law does (Romans 3:20)—and therefore open up the possibility of repentance. They are also relevant to the life of the repentant believer whose nature is being changed through the process of sanctification, a process in which you become able to keep the commandments through the workings of grace.

mercy on them. The plan of redemption, then, is about mercy. To make sense of what human action opens up the possibility of this mercy, we need to have an understanding of what repentance is. Alma's own experience is relevant here. He says that after three days of being in intense spiritual pain, he remembered the teachings about Christ and called upon him: "I cried within my heart: O Jesus, thou Son of God, have mercy on me" (Alma 36:18). After this, he was no longer harrowed up by the memory of his sins. It is striking how simple this was. He cried for mercy, and it was granted. There is no mention of anything like restitution—and this was clearly not contingent on good works, which he had yet to perform.

While Alma's story is unusually dramatic, it is not unique in the Book of Mormon. The people of King Benjamin, for example, go through a similar process. First, they view themselves in their sinful state. Then they cry for mercy, grounded in their belief in Christ: "O have *mercy* and apply the atoning blood of Christ that we may receive forgiveness of our sins" (Mosiah 4:2). The story of Zeezrom in Alma 15 also follows this pattern: he is tormented by awareness of sin and then healed through his belief in Christ. Repentance, rather than involving elaborate steps, might be as simple as coming to an awareness of your sins and calling to God for mercy.

Repentance is the active requirement to obtain mercy. There is also a passive one: do not be hard-hearted. What does that mean? One scriptural way of understanding it is being unable to be entreated, unresponsive. This is the case in the classic story of hard-heartedness, in which Pharaoh refuses to let the children of Israel go, no matter what Moses and Aaron do. The term is used in this sense many times in the Book of Mormon. In 3 Nephi, for example, the people who are described as hard-hearted begin "to be less and less astonished at a sign or a wonder from heaven" (3 Nephi 2:1). Nephi, the son of Helaman, understands hardening your heart in terms of not hearkening—in this case, to "the voice of the Good Shepherd" (Helaman 7:18). The members of the evil church that eventually develops in 4 Nephi "harden their hearts" despite miracles and "seek to kill" the disciples of Jesus (4 Nephi 1:31). Laman and Lemuel would also exemplify those who are described as hard-hearted despite having heard the word of the Lord and even seeing an angel (1 Nephi 7:8–10).

In all this, hardening the heart involves resisting the influence of something divine manifested in a person's life, whether it be miracles from God or even just the power of the word. In talking about his own experience of hard-heartedness, Amulek says, "I was called many times and I would not hear" (Alma 10:6). The injunction not to be hard-hearted therefore assumes that God is somehow acting in our lives. King Benjamin, we might recall, speaks of yielding "to the enticings of the Holy Spirit" (Mosiah 3:19). God reaches out to us. What is required of us is to be responsive. Repentance and not being hard-hearted are two halves of the same coin: if we let God's reaching out affect us, we will repent; and if we repent, we will be open to responding to God's reaching out. This is where agency plays a role—in our ability to respond to God's call to us and not be hard-hearted and in our ability to repent and call on God for mercy. Given that it is God's actions that make this situation possible, one can say that grace enables and shapes human freedom. God's call creates the human situation in the sense that it sets out our choices: to accept grace or reject it.

One could make the case, however, that Alma 13 calls into question the model outlined here. The priests in this chapter, like all of us, were "left to choose good or evil"—and they chose good (Alma 13:3). Alma also speaks of their "righteousness before God" (v. 10), and their "exceeding faith and good works" (v. 3). How is this not an instance of someone exercising a Pelagian freedom to do good? For one thing, I think, there is no indication that these people have escaped the effects of the fall. And as Mosiah's son Aaron observes, "Since man had fallen he could not merit any thing of himself" (Alma 22:14). I think the relevant question is, then, What does it mean to choose good in a fallen state?

The definitive characteristic of these priests—what distinguishes them from those who do not receive this calling—is lack of hard-heartedness (Alma 13:4–5). Put another way, they have chosen to yield to the influence of grace. The freedom we do have in our fallen state, if we go back to Lehi's blessing of Jacob, is to choose "liberty and eternal life" through Christ, or the "captivity and death" of the devil (2 Nephi 2:27). This is genuine freedom. But crucially, it is not the same as the freedom to do good, which requires a reorientation of the will that is brought about by grace, specifically by the workings of the Spirit. It is important to note that these priests are said to have been "sanctified by the Holy Ghost" (Alma 13:12). Righteousness is an effect of this process of repentance and not being hard-hearted—not a prerequisite for mercy.

I have talked a fair amount here about the conditions that allow us to access mercy. I would now like to touch on wrath. As noted above, it is interesting that mercy and wrath are the opposing forces here, rather than mercy and justice. Might the reference to wrath instead of justice have to do with the audience? In Alma 42, where he explicates the relationship between justice and mercy, Alma is speaking to his son Corianton, who specifically has a concern about God's justice in punishing the sinner (Alma 42:1). The people of Ammonihah, as mentioned earlier, are Nehorite universalists. Nehor taught that humans "need not fear nor tremble," as all were redeemed (Alma 1:4). Alma, then, is not tasked with the complexities of relating justice to mercy, but of warning that not only mercy, but wrath as well, is a real attribute of God—and that one should not take redemption for granted, for it will be denied to those with hard hearts.

This text has a close relationship to Hebrews. Hebrews 3 relates how the children of Israel hardened their hearts, and God swore in his wrath that they should not enter into his rest and left them in the wilderness for forty years. In other words, they were punished with temporal death. In Alma 12:36, Alma speaks of the "first provocation" in which God sent down his wrath, possibly referring to this story of the children of Israel—which is indeed called "the provocation" in Hebrews 3:8, as well as in Jacob 1:7. One might also make the case that the "first provocation" here refers to the fall, given the use of the term *first* and the fact that the fall has already come up in this chapter. But either way, the penalty is exile and death. Alma then goes on to warn of the "last provocation," which will also bring God's wrath, and something more terrifying than temporal death: "the everlasting destruction of your souls" (Alma 12:36). What is it exactly that provokes God's wrath and leads to these disturbing consequences? It is hardening one's heart and engaging in iniquity that are the problem. Again, there is something passive and something active—resisting God's call, on the one hand, and doing evil, on the other. And just as God reaches out to influence human choice, so does the devil: the Book of Mormon speaks of "yielding" to sin, temptation, and the devil (2 Nephi 4:27; Mormon 9:28; Alma 5:20). If we give way to these things, we are subject to divine wrath, which is contrasted to both mercy and rest.

How are mercy and wrath related? There is a sense in which they appear to be equivalent, in that they are set up in contrast with each other. But looking at the situation more closely, mercy is primary. As mentioned, the plan of redemption shows up first, and only then does God give commandments, the violation of which sparks wrath. The discussion of hard-heartedness also illuminates this dynamic—God in his mercy reaches out to humans, and it is up to humans to respond. It is only if we fail to be influenced by this initial move by God that wrath kicks in. Notably, in the repentance stories I mentioned, God is described as immediately responding to cries for mercy, but his wrath is not said to be immediate, as humans are given a space for repentance. One could also say that the very preaching of God's wrath is actually an instance of his mercy, as humans are thereby warned of the consequences of not repenting and given an opportunity to turn to God. Mercy is thus more fundamental.

In conclusion, mercy is available to humans if we will repent and not harden our hearts. If we do this, we are promised the rest of the Lord. If we do not, we are subject to his wrath. Our most basic choice is not between some kind of abstract good and evil, but the choice of whether to respond to God's reaching out to us or to resist his grace and thereby provoke him. Alma's message here is one of warning, but it is also one of hope and possibility.

Seams, Cracks, and Fragments: Notes on the Human Condition

Joseph M. Spencer

According to the Book of Mormon, seams and cracks and fragments serve as geological witnesses to the plan of redemption. Nephi captures this idea early in the book in a kind of theological formula. "The rocks of the earth must rend," he says, when "the god of nature suffers" (1 Nephi 19:12). Apparently for this reason, what before the death of Christ was "one solid mass" of stone has since been—and is apparently "ever after" to be—"found in seams and in cracks and in broken fragments upon the face of the whole earth" (Helaman 14:21–22). Of this Samuel prophesies a few years before the birth of Christ, and then Mormon reports some chapters later that, although "the earth did" eventually "cleave together again" after Christ's death (3 Nephi 10:10), "the rocks" were nonetheless irreversibly rent, such that "they were found in broken fragments and in seams and in cracks upon all the face of the land" (3 Nephi 8:18). Highlighting the fact that these geological phenomena bear witness of the plan of redemption, Mormon urges his readers to "search" the scriptures to "see and behold" if "all these things are not unto the fulfilling of the prophecies of many of the holy prophets" (3 Nephi 10:14).

This material geotheology in the Book of Mormon runs parallel to a formal cosmotheology spelled out in the volume—or so I have come to think as I have worked on Alma 12–13 in conversation with my fellow seminarians. Just as Christ's actual death rends the one solid mass of rock, making it a matter of seams and cracks and fragments, Christ's virtual death, his being "slain from the foundation of the world" (Revelation 13:8), rends *eternity* and gives rise to *time*, which is characterized by its own seams and cracks and fragments. In both cases, both the geological and the cosmological, Christ's death and the possibility of redemption break up the continuous and leave us with the discrete. But further, because Alma outlines his understanding of the relationship between time and eternity most fully in the course of responding to a question about the human condition (see Alma 12:20–21), a certain anthropotheology (a theological account of human nature) mirrors his cosmotheology (his theological account of time and eternity). Alma arguably understands human beings, those most time bound of all creatures, as finding *themselves* only in seams and cracks and fragments. The cherubim who guard the way to the tree of life (see v. 21) serve as scriptural ciphers for the fracture of eternity, but also for the split that divides human beings against themselves.

In this paper, I wish primarily to develop just the last of these three theologies: Alma's anthropotheology. The body of the paper is therefore given to this task. Beyond that, however, I wish to develop at least in outline Alma's cosmotheology as well. Because of the technical nature of that task, and because I wish to do it more briefly, I have relegated this second task to an appendix, following the main argument of the paper. (As for the Book of Mormon's geotheology, because it does not derive from Alma 12–13, I leave its elaboration for another occasion, drawing from it only a guiding image for this paper: that of seams and cracks and fragments.) Although I displace my elaboration of Alma's cosmotheology into an appendix, I would like to note that I take it to be intertwined with—or at least in a mirroring relationship to—his anthropotheology. A fuller elaboration of the connection, however, awaits another opportunity.

Twice in the course of Alma 12–13 Alma focuses directly on the question of human nature. The first, which appears in Alma 12:24, briefly presents the human condition as "a probationary state," "a time to prepare." According to this passage, the human condition is bounded at its horizon by "the temporal death," but it is also oriented beyond that horizon to an "endless state" that comes "after the resurrection of the dead." Elsewhere in this volume, Adam Miller provides a beautiful analysis of this and related texts within Alma's discourse. I am quite happy to leave verse 24's theological exposition to him while focusing my attention more or less solely on the second of Alma's two discussions of human nature. That second discussion appears in Alma 12:31, a brief aside within a larger passage focused on God's having given commandments to human beings after their exile from Eden. The verse opens with a reference to this giving of commandments, but then it diverts itself by attempting to describe the basic motivations for God's giving of commandments. That motivation is, summarily put, the human condition itself. "Men," Alma says, "transgressed the first commandments" given to them: their instructions not to eat from the tree of knowledge. And the consequence was that they became human; they became the sort of creature we still are today. It was for this reason that "God gave unto them commandments" (v. 32).

What does the human condition, as Alma describes it, look like? Unfortunately, there is no simple answer to that question, at the very least because there are several quite distinct ways Alma 12:31 can be read. And crucially, none of the several possible readings should be preferred over the others solely on syntactical grounds. To decide among possible interpretations of Alma's description of the human condition is to make a *theological* decision, a decision for one reading over another because one wishes to pursue the theological implications of that reading. It seems to me best to lay out three possible interpretations of the text before pursuing the one that seems to me the most theologically promising.

Here is the description of the human condition from Alma 12:31, presented without punctuation (it should be remembered that Joseph Smith did not dictate punctuation along with the words of the Book of Mormon):

> becoming as Gods knowing good from evil placing themselves in a state to act or being placed in a state to act according to their wills and pleasures whether to do evil or to do good

Interpretation of these words, it seems to me, turns on the scope and function of the *or* that appears more or less at the center of the text. Both the scope and function of this *or* deserve some description and development.

By scope, I refer to how many phrases the *or* in Alma 12:31 connects. Does the *or* simply connect "placing themselves in a state to act" with "being placed in a state to act"? If so, the later phrase, "according to their wills and pleasures," would qualify both instances of the verb "to act." This first possibility might be represented by the following approach to punctuating the text:

> becoming as Gods, knowing good from evil, placing themselves in a state to act (or being placed in a state to act) according to their wills and pleasures—whether to do evil or to do good

A second option would be to assume that the *or* connects all the phrases following in verse 31, from "being placed in a state to act" onward—with the implication that everything following the *or* is presented as an alternative to everything that precedes the *or*. This might be represented by a rather different approach to punctuating the text (even inserting some bracketed numbers to signal the alternatives presented):

> [1] becoming as Gods, knowing good from evil, placing themselves in a state to act, *or* [2] being placed in a state to act according to their wills and pleasures, whether to do evil or to do good

These two approaches cover the range of options as regards the scope of the *or* in Alma 12:31.

Before turning to the question of the function of the *or*, I might note that the first of the above two approaches to the scope of the *or* is by far the more familiar—and perhaps in some sense the more natural—of the two. The fact that "in a state to act" appears immediately following both "placing themselves" and "or being placed" certainly makes the reader feel as if, once she has come to the end of the repetition of "in a state to act," she has caught back up to the point where the *or* interrupts the flow of the text. She therefore naturally assumes that the interruption has run its course by that point and that the scope of the *or* extends only to "being placed in a state to act." But, however familiar this approach to the text might be, and however natural it might in some sense feel, it must be emphasized that nothing in the syntax of the passage requires that it be read this way. It is entirely possible, syntactically speaking, that the reader is presented with alternative descriptions of some "state to act," one description before and the other description after the *or.* Any decision in favor of either interpretation of the scope of the *or* must be decided on theological grounds.

Next, by function, I refer to the question of whether the *or* is inclusive or exclusive—that is, whether it presents alternatives that might both be true, or whether it presents alternatives, only one of which may be true. The inclusive use of the word *or* is exemplified in a sentence like "Karen or Kim will suggest a good place to eat." This sentence would not turn out to be false if both Karen and Kim make suggestions about where to eat, but neither would it turn out to be false if only one of the two makes a suggestion. It is in this sense that this sentence's *or* is inclusive; the truth of one alternative does not preclude the truth of the other alternative presented. By contrast, the exclusive use of the word *or* is exemplified in a sentence like the following: "Either Jenny or Sharon will get the last available seat at the restaurant." Here the truth of the sentence depends on only one of the two alternative situations proving to be the case; if both Jenny and Sharon were to get the last seat, the sentence would turn out to be false (just as it would if neither got the last seat). This sentence's *or* is exclusive. The question of the function of the *or* in Alma 12:31 thus means to ask whether the alternatives marked by the *or* (whatever the scope of the *or* may be) should be understood as presenting rival or consonant possibilities. Does the *or* mean to present the same idea in two distinct ways, or does the *or* mean to present ultimately inconsistent ideas?

This question of function might seem abstract at first. But its significance becomes much clearer when it is brought to bear on the text of Alma 12:31. I will, over the next several pages, outline three distinct interpretations of this verse in light of the scope and the function of the *or*. These will clarify greatly the stakes of inclusive and exclusive interpretations of the term.

A first interpretation of Alma 12:31 would understand the scope of the *or* to be limited to "being placed in a state to act," and it would understand the function of the *or* to be exclusive. This might be called the "corrective" interpretation, because it takes the interjection of the *or* (along with what it covers) as intended to correct a mistake. On this interpretation, Alma (or the narrator, or the editor, or perhaps even the translator) spoke (or wrote) too quickly at first, infelicitously attributing to Eve and Adam the Godlike ability to *place themselves* in a state to act. From this perspective, it would be true enough that Adam and Eve became "as Gods" and came to know "good from evil," but it would be wrong to think that they could "plac[e] themselves in a state to act." Who could believe that the first human beings had any such power of self-determination? Luckily, Alma (or the narrator, editor, or translator) immediately recognized the error and corrected it by saying (or writing): "or, *being placed* in a state to act." The clear trace of the error, however, remains present in the final form of the text.

This corrective interpretation clearly limits the scope of the *or* since it understands only the words "being placed in a state to act" (not the remainder of the verse) to be required to correct the inadvertent error; the original thought about being "in a state to act" resumes immediately after the corrective clause, beginning with the words "according to." Further, this interpretation clearly regards the function of the *or* to be exclusive, because it sees talk of Eve and Adam's "being placed in a state to act" as true to the exclusion of any talk of them "placing themselves in a state to act." Ultimately, on this first interpretation, the appearance of the *or* in the verse is largely unfortunate and accidental—or perhaps instructive. Some who espouse the corrective approach would certainly think that it would have been preferable if the mistake had never been made—that is, if the verse had read simply as follows: "becoming as Gods, knowing good from evil, . . . being placed in a state to act according to their wills and pleasures, whether to do evil or to do good." Others espousing this interpretation, however, might regard the retention of the error in the text as deliberate or at least useful; it potentially makes clear to readers the theological error of thinking that the first human beings had any power of self-determination. Either way, adherents of this first interpretation would certainly wish to say that only one of the two alternatives—specifically that following the *or*—is true.

A second interpretation of Alma 12:31 would similarly understand the scope of the *or* to be limited to "being placed in a state to act," but it would understand the function of the *or* to be inclusive rather than exclusive. This interpretation might be called the "synthetic" interpretation, because it advocates the idea that it is impossible to assign with accuracy either activity or passivity to Adam and Eve at the moment they entered the human condition. This approach, which is represented in some of the other papers in this collection, sees a paradox at work in the beginnings of human agency. It would seem ultimately inappropriate to say that Eve and Adam actively placed themselves in a state to act, since then they would have to have acted before they were in a state to do so. At the same time, it would seem just as inappropriate to say that they were passively placed in a state to act, since they could only come into such a state by deliberately eating from the tree of knowledge. Agency would thus appear to have its beginnings in a necessarily paradoxical leap. The world as we know it—divided into "things to act" and "things to be acted upon" (2 Nephi 2:14)—arose out of an event that, because the fundamental division between activity and passivity was its result, cannot itself be properly described in either active or passive terms. But we have no other choice in using language than to use active or passive terms. Hence, according to this second interpretation, Alma describes the origins of human agency by describing it twice—once in active language ("placing themselves in a state to act") and once in passive language ("being placed in a state to act").

This, then, is the synthetic approach, which sees Alma synthesizing the active and the passive in order to highlight the inappropriateness of either kind of language for describing the origins of agency. It, like the corrective interpretation, limits the scope of the *or* in Alma 12:31, since it assumes that the active and passive alternatives concern just the arrival of Adam and Eve in "a state to act"; the *or* in no way concerns the remainder of the verse. But this interpretation differs from the first because it understands the function of the *or* to be inclusive. That is, the synthetic approach understands "placing themselves in a state to act" and "being placed in a state to act" as alternative expressions of one and the same (inexpressible) idea. The two might be true together (however paradoxical that seems from our present perspective), or, better, the two are ultimately false or at least misleading together. For this reason, this second interpretation differs from the first in another way. Where the corrective interpretation regards the presence of the *or* as largely unfortunate and accidental (or perhaps, by way of its mistake, as instructive), the synthetic interpretation regards the use of the *or* as essential to communicating the truth of the matter. The *or* allows for a formulation of the paradoxical origins of agency, one that does not misconstrue—or at least comes close to not misconstruing—the nature of such origins.

Now, despite the important differences just discussed, these first two interpretations of the *or*-clause in Alma 12:31 have much in common. Obviously, as I have already emphasized, they share an interpretation of the scope of the *or*, despite their distinct approaches to its function. But this point of similarity has larger interpretive consequences. In the end, it must be said that there is no real difference in these first two approaches' understandings of the human condition. This is because what distinguishes these first two approaches from each other is not their respective views of human nature but rather their respective views of how human beings *come into* human nature. They differ only on the relationship between the two phrases "placing themselves" and "being placed." For both, the *or* in Alma 12:31 only briefly interrupts an otherwise seamless presentation of human nature—whether to correct a misconstrual of God's role in producing human nature (the corrective interpretation) or to underscore the paradoxical leap involved in the emergence of human nature (the synthetic interpretation). Consequently, for both of these first two approaches to the text, human nature is simply that "state to act" where human beings are "as Gods, knowing good from evil" and fully able "to act according to their wills and pleasures, whether to do evil or to do good." That is, for every interpretation that limits the scope of the *or*, the human condition is a Godlike (but nonetheless nondivine) condition of *knowing* and *doing*—of knowing good and evil, and of being able to act by doing good or evil.

Because the corrective and the synthetic interpretations of Alma 12:31 share a basic understanding of human nature, one that assumes a certain continuity between knowledge and ability to act, it seems relatively clear what it would mean to construct a theological anthropology beginning from either of these two approaches to the text: one would have to proceed to investigate as probingly as possible the apparent continuity between knowing and doing, when it comes to good and evil. But, for reasons Sheila Taylor spells out in more detail in her contribution to this volume, I must confess that claims of supposed continuity between knowing and doing make me theologically suspicious. These first two interpretations seem to me too Pelagian, too convinced that human agency is sufficient to itself—as if *knowing* did not in fact more or less constantly get in the way of *doing*. My experience has consistently left me to find myself only in the seams and cracks and fragments of any supposed continuity between knowing and doing. Human nature, before or apart from or resistant to its redemption in the Messiah's grace, seems to me always to be *divided between* knowing and doing, rather than *situated at the point of their coincidence*.

Something like what I have just described certainly seems to characterize the experience of the apostle Paul. In one of Paul's most famous texts, one finds a poignant expression of radical discontinuity between knowing and doing. Knowing the good, and even wanting it, is not enough to make it possible to do it. As in Alma's words, Paul's text focuses on the moment when God "gave commandments unto men" (Alma 12:31). And Paul directly connects the commandments to knowledge of good and evil: "If it had not been for the law, I would not have known sin" (Romans 7:7 NRSV). But as soon as the commandments assist Paul in knowing good and evil—as soon as he can "agree that the law is good" (v. 16)—he finds that he cannot bring his actions into conformity with what he knows to be good. "I do not do what I want, but I do the very thing I hate," he says (v. 15); "I can will what is right, but I cannot do it. For I do not do the good I want, but the evil I do not want is what I do" (vv. 18–19). The frustration Paul experiences in connection with this ongoing state of affairs leads him to near despair: "Wretched man that I am!" he exclaims (v. 24).

Paul is hardly alone, as any reader of the Book of Mormon knows. Nephi expresses the same self-doubt and makes the same self-critical exclamation: "Notwithstanding the great goodness of the Lord in shewing me his great and marvelous works—my heart exclaimeth: O wretched man that I am!" (2 Nephi 4:17). He goes on: "When I desire to rejoice, my heart groaneth because of my sins" (v. 19); and he finds he has to ask himself "why" he should "weep" and "linger in the valley of sorrow" and "waste away" and "slacken" and become "angry because of [his] enemy" (vv. 26–27). Nephi, like Paul, suggests that knowledge of the good, far from simply enabling one then to set about doing good, more often than not reveals just how disinclined one naturally is to doing good. And this is something Nephi might well have learned from his father, Lehi, who claims that "men are instructed sufficiently that they know good from evil" in that "the law is given" to them, but by this knowledge-granting law "no flesh is justified" and "men are cut off" (2 Nephi 2:5). In the end, numerous scriptural voices give us reason to think that there is a fundamental *disjunction* between knowing good and evil and having the ability to do good or evil.

Perhaps Alma feels the same way. If he does, or if the passages just discussed give us motivation enough to explore the possibility that he does, then we might venture to interpret the *or* of Alma 12:31 in a way quite distinct from that of the corrective and synthetic approaches. This third approach would understand the scope of the *or* of our text to extend to the conclusion of the verse, rather than just to the end of the clause "being placed in a state to act." And it would understand the function of the *or* to be exclusive, rather than inclusive, as if the verse means to outline alternative possibilities that cannot both be true (or, in this case, false) at the same time. This third approach might rightly be termed the "parallax" interpretation. According to it, the text disjoins or—at least in the last instance—renders discontinuous *knowing* good and evil and the ability to *do* good or evil. That is, the *or* here presents us with a forced alternative. This forced alternative needs some articulation. And here I might simply describe my own representative experience—fundamentally similar to what I see Paul, Nephi, and Lehi describing. In setting such a description forth, however, I will limit myself to the language and ideas of Alma 12:31.

In my fallen or my lost situation, I invariably find myself alternating between two mutually exclusive "states." On the one hand or at certain moments, I find myself in the state of possessing Godlike knowledge and being able to determine my intentions. That is, at times I find that we human beings have "become as Gods, knowing good from evil, placing ourselves in a state to act." A kind of euphoria or even delirium attaches itself to this state. The clarity with which I can see the world reaches to the heavens, and I can deliberate decisively about what I ought to do with myself. Yet, to the extent that I find myself in this first state, I find also that I am entirely unable to do the good or the evil that I see with such clarity and in terms of which I wish desperately to determine myself. I know exactly what I ought or what I wish to do, but I find that I cannot actually do it. Although I place myself in a state to act, my actions end up unaligned with my will and disconnected from any pleasure I might take in deliberately doing good or evil. I know the good, and I wish to do it, but I find myself being selfish and vindictive. I fall devastatingly short of what I can outline in my mind perfectly well. In short, precisely to the extent that I see human beings as knowing good and evil, I find that we *cannot* "act according to [our] wills and pleasures, whether to do evil or to do good."

This first state is nicely illustrated by the situation in which Eve and Adam found themselves immediately after eating the fruit of the tree of knowledge. At that moment, they saw for the first time their nakedness, and they knew shame. Each felt responsible before the other for the first time, but what each felt responsible *for* was something over which she or he had no real or at least no ultimate control: her or his *body*. They had been granted Godlike knowledge, but the result was that—although they could see everything with perfect clarity—suddenly, they could not do much of anything, except perhaps awkwardly (certainly never with any real grace). And in fact, there is no better way to end up entirely unable to act than to be fully self-conscious, fully aware of being in a situation where it is necessary to act while awaiting the judgment of others. The fact is that the more fully knowledgeable we are about things, and therefore the more deeply aware we are of the infinite complexity of things, the more we find ourselves immobilized, unable to do anything at all.

But then, on the other hand or at certain other moments, I find myself in a rather different state: a state where I am fully capable of getting things done, taking real pleasure in what I do and experiencing no hindrance to my will. That is, at times I find that we human beings can in fact "act according to our wills and pleasures, whether to do evil or to do good." A rather different sort of euphoria or delirium descends on me when I find myself in this state. My ability to act appears boundless, and real pleasure attends my actions. Yet, to the extent that I find myself in this second state, I find also that I am entirely ignorant of what in my actions really serves the good and what ultimately serves the purposes of evil—and I experience a kind of all-too-human feeling of impotence. I do exactly as I wish, and deep feelings come over me unbidden, but I have no idea how to decide whether what I am doing is what I ought to be doing. Although I exercise my will and experience pleasure, I suffer desire passively, as a foreign imposition, and I feel that I could not be more unlike a heavenly being. I do good and evil, but I find that I fail to understand what I am doing. In short, precisely to the extent that I see human beings as doing good or evil, I find that we *have not* "[become] as Gods, knowing good from evil."

This second state is nicely illustrated by what Jesus Christ describes as happening at the end of time, when the final judgment arrives. Whether we find ourselves at his left hand or at his right, he says, we will be told that we did good or evil *without* knowing it. "When saw we thee an hungered . . . ? or thirsty . . . ? When saw we thee a stranger . . . ? or naked . . . ? Or when saw we thee sick, or in prison . . . ?" (Matthew 25:37–39). From Jesus's parable, it would seem that the righteous and the wicked alike have little understanding of what they do. From the cross, in fact, Jesus pleads for our collective forgiveness because we "know not what [we] do" (Luke 23:34). At the final judgment, when everything can be seen for what it really is, we will apparently learn that we have been rather poor at guessing at our real motivations. If we try to make honest sense of even half of what we do, we must confess that we often make mere conjectures about our reasons for doing things, and we are wrong about much or most of it. And, of course, it is unquestionably true that every time we wish to think carefully about our actions, we must *stop* acting in order to do so. Inevitably, we act in ignorance, letting thought and reflection fall to the wayside while we attempt to get things done.

Here, then, is the human condition according to the parallax interpretation of Alma 12:31. The *or* at the heart of the verse radically divides knowing from doing, and doing from knowing. It fractures human being at its very core, in parallel to the fracturing of eternity that produces the time in which human being unfolds. Trapped in time, we discover that the more we know, the more impotent we are, and that the more we can do, the less we can make sense of what we do. At any given moment, we sustain *some* kind of relation to good and evil, and we are in *some* sort of "state to act." But the question at any given moment is whether our relation to good and evil is principally a matter of knowledge (in which case we are guaranteed infinite frustration at our inability to do what we know we ought, despite placing ourselves in a state to act) *or* whether our relation to good and evil is principally a matter of action (in which case we are guaranteed infinite frustration at our inability to understand what we do, since we have been alienatingly placed in a state to act).

Knowingly impotent or ignorantly active—we alternate between these two inconsistent "states." *That* is the human condition.

I cannot help but wonder whether this strict divide between knowing and doing, glimpsed in the third possible interpretation of Alma 12:31 (the parallax interpretation), helps to make sense of Alma's description of the human condition as "preparatory." I said before that I am happy to leave the interpretation of Alma's other brief discussion of the human condition, found in Alma 12:24, to Adam Miller. But perhaps I might add just one comment to Miller's rich analysis. Why do we, as fallen human beings, spend our time preparing? Might it not be a way of compensating for the dilemma I have attempted to articulate above? In preparing, we pretend that the divide between knowing and doing is simply a *temporal* divide, a divide between before and after. We work on knowing *now*, pretending that we will thus be ready to do something *later*. And thus, in our preparations, we pretend that *we* are the ones who divide knowing from doing, as if we *intentionally* separate knowing from doing so as to make the former's exhaustive execution the gateway to successful accomplishment of the latter. But this is, of course, sheer fantasy, pretending that the void that traumatically divides us from ourselves is really just a feature of our own brilliant strategizing about how to do things in the best way possible. Ultimately, this fantasy just masks our procrastination. Generally speaking, we prepare so that we do not have to be redeemed. Or better, we prepare so that we can ignore the fact that we have always already been redeemed, according to the redemption that was prepared from the foundation of the world.

Until we give up and allow God, at last, to redeem us, we are condemned to endless preparation. In the human—the *unredeemed*—condition, we are fragmented and cracked, just like eternity in the Book of Mormon's cosmotheology and the rocks in the Book of Mormon's geotheology. But then there is the possibility of redemption. And in redemption, the *or* of Alma 12:31 might assume a fourth meaning: one where its scope is as broad as in the third or parallax approach, but one also where its function is inclusive rather than exclusive. In redemption, it might at last be true *both* that we know *and* that we act. The fragments that result from the crack at the heart of human nature might be sewn together in a seam. In redemption, we might concede Alma's radical disjunction, the fracture between knowing and doing. But we might at the same time receive both our impotent knowing and our ignorant doing as things that work together for good. We remain cracked, and our parts remain fragments, but a seam stitches us together in a way that good becomes possible.

God has been preparing us for just such a possibility since the foundation of the world. And we are likely to bear the scars of our passage through the human condition not only for time but for all eternity.

Appendix: Alma's Cosmotheology

The time of the world, according to Alma, begins with a seminal event or series of events, to which he returns again and again in his discourse in Alma 12–13. He illuminatingly assigns this event or series of events to an inaugural temporal moment, which he consistently calls "the foundation of the world." At no point does Alma pause to describe this event or series of events in systematic fashion or sustained detail. Instead, he refers to it only occasionally, providing mere glimpses of its basic nature. It seems, though, according to his account, to have been primarily a matter of *preparation*, since Alma refers to several things that were "prepared from the foundation of the world." These include "the plan of redemption" (Alma 12:30), "priests" who are both "called" and prepared (Alma 13:2–3), and a certain "holy calling" (v. 5). Hence, whatever else might have taken place at the foundation of the world, Alma clearly believes that a good deal of *preparatory* work was accomplished then.

As if to underscore the importance of preparation in each of these passages, the several prepared things Alma mentions *look forward* in one way or another—and each looks forward always, significantly, toward redemption. The plan of redemption, the first thing Alma mentions as having been prepared from the foundation of the world, is in and of itself clearly provisionary, looking forward to what Christ would accomplish. As for the second thing Alma attaches to the foundation of the world—priests called and prepared at that time—he says they are ordained typologically, such that "the people might know in what manner to look forward . . . for redemption" (Alma 13:2). And finally, the holy calling Alma also says was prepared from the foundation of the world was, he claims, prepared "with and according to a preparatory redemption" for those who receive it (v. 3). Hence, all things prepared from the foundation of the world can be said, from Alma's perspective, to have been laid out "according to the foreknowledge of God" (v. 3).

It seems safe to say that, if Alma indeed believes that time interrupts eternity, it is the event or the series of events taking place at the foundation of the world that "initially" accomplishes this interruption. And thus the world and its time, separated out from eternity, find their foundation in *preparation.* Timeless eternity fractures and fragments from the moment that something is *prepared.* One might in fact say that preparation necessarily fractures and then fragments eternity because the preparatory looks forward from one time to another, provisionally. To put the point formulaically, time supplants eternity through preparation—even though what is prepared for, in all of Alma's talk about the foundation of the world, is redemption. One might say that redemption dawns as a possibility only where eternity gives way to time, that is, where life becomes first and foremost a "preparatory state" (Alma 12:26) rather than a kind of continuous existence.

Now, these are suggestive ways of reading Alma's text, but one might well wonder whether they are really justified. What justifies this interpretation in my mind is a further passage, Alma 13:7, where Alma once more refers—*but in a fundamentally distinct way*—to the foundation of the world. In this further passage, he refers to something he consistently regards as eternal, rather than to something he regards as having had its preparatory beginnings only at the foundation of the world. That is, where in previous passages Alma speaks of things that were apparently ordained only in the course of the event or series of events that took place at the foundation of the world, in this further passage he speaks of something that apparently already *was* when that event or series of events "initially" interrupted eternity. The plan of redemption, priests themselves, and the holy calling: these all had their beginnings at the foundation of the world. But *the holy order,* or "the order of [God's] Son," Alma explicitly describes as "being without beginning of days or end of years" (v. 7). The holy order is eternal, *not* prepared from the foundation of the world. And yet Alma *does,* as he goes on, nonetheless connect the holy order to *both* preparation *and* the foundation of the world. But he makes these connections in an odd way, thus distinguishing the holy order from the callings and priests and plan that were all "prepared from the foundation of the world."

In effect, when speaking of the holy order, Alma separates "preparation" from "the foundation of the world." The holy order is, like all the other things Alma talks about, something *prepared,* but it was not prepared *from the foundation of the world.* While the holy order is in some way oriented to *the foundation of the world,* that orientation is in no way one of *having been prepared at that time.* What Alma says is simply that the holy order "*was* from the foundation of the world," and that it is "prepared *from eternity to all eternity*" (Alma 13:7). Each of the two parts of Alma's usual formula ("being prepared," "from the foundation of the world") is in Alma 13:7 separated from the other and attached to something else (the one to "from eternity to all eternity," the other simply to "was").

Alma 12:30: "the plan of redemption which had *been prepared from the foundation of the world*"

Alma 13:2–3: "priests . . . *being* called and *prepared from the foundation of the world*"

Alma 13:5: "this holy calling *being prepared from the foundation of the world*"

"BEING PREPARED *from the foundation of the world*"

Alma 13:7: "the order of his Son, which order was *from the foundation of the world*—or in other words, being without beginning of days or end of years, *being prepared from eternity to all eternity*, according to his foreknowledge of all things"

"was *from the foundation of the world*"

"BEING PREPARED from eternity to all eternity"

Clearly, Alma wishes his hearers and, eventually, his readers to understand that the holy order is in some fundamental way distinct from the other things he discusses. It is eternal, and so its relationship both to preparation and to the foundation of the world is unique.

What is most theologically intriguing in Alma 13:7 is Alma's odd claim that the holy order is "prepared from eternity to all eternity." At one level, the formula just seems paradoxical, as if it made sense to speak of something *being prepared eternally*. At another level, however, the formula might be interpreted as itself pointing to the fracturing and fragmentation of eternity. In the formula, perhaps, one might discern *eternity dividing itself*, dividing itself into "eternity" and "all eternity"—the former open and oriented (the order is prepared *from* eternity) and the latter complete and at rest (the order is prepared *to* all eternity). Perhaps provisional plans and typological ordinations and preparatory redemptions take initial shape inasmuch as God's eternal order, without beginning of days or end of years, finds its place in time somewhere between "eternity" and "all eternity." Thus, at the foundation of the world, when many other preparatory things had their beginnings, the eternal order opened a seam or produced a crack in eternity and therefore assumed a kind of preparatory shape. The holy order, eternal rather than provisionary, nonetheless gives itself over to "being prepared" as eternity divides itself into eternity *before* (not yet finished, not yet "all") and eternity *after* (apparently total, "all eternity").

If this interpretation is not too far off the track, then it might be said that Alma 13:7 understands time to follow a kind of movement toward wholeness, toward "all eternity" and "according to [God's] foreknowledge of all things." Perhaps time is a kind of detotalization of eternity that then organizes a movement—through so much preparation—toward retotalization or renewed wholeness. Incidentally, the apostle Paul seems to say something quite similar. Paul sees time as a melee, over the course of which "all enemies" must be put down—"the last" of which is "death" (1 Corinthians 15:25–26). And he says that this whole process comes to an end, time finally giving way to eternity anew, when God is at last "all in all" (v. 28). It may well be that Alma shares this Pauline conviction, anticipating in eternity the becoming whole of what for the moment is only partial. "When that which is perfect is come, then that which is in part shall be done away" (1 Corinthians 13:10).

A Preparatory Redemption

Adam S. Miller

It is hard to sit still. Have you noticed this?

It's hard to sit at a desk and work. It's hard to pray and remember what you were saying. It's hard to listen to your child. It's hard to put away your phone. Impatience is an itch. It's like a little house fire, shut up in your muscles and bones. It curls your toes and taps your foot and makes you toss and turn in bed.

This itch, this little fire in your bones, is the mind. There's something about mind itself that refuses to rest. There is something about mind that's geared for action, that's always planning the next thing, always worrying about or hoping for the next thing. There is something about mind that can't stop looking forward, that just wants to act already and not be acted upon.

It's fair to call this mind. But we might just as fairly call it agency. Agency is grounded in this perpetual looking forward, this endless hoping and planning, this burning itch to go somewhere and to do something, this hunger to expend energy, exercise power, and act. Thus, as minded agents, we find ourselves always in a perpetual state of preparation. We find ourselves always getting ready for something else.

A preparatory state

This, Alma tells the people of Ammonihah, is what defines the human condition. "Having first transgressed the first commandments" that were given in Eden, our first parents ended up "becoming as Gods, knowing good from evil, placing themselves in a state to act, or being placed in a state to act according to their wills and pleasures, whether to do evil or to do good" (Alma 12:31). Then, finding themselves in this state to act, life itself becomes "a probationary state, a time to prepare to meet God, a time to prepare for that endless state . . . which is after the resurrection of the dead" (v. 24).

Though it is certainly true that our first parents "would have been forever miserable, having no preparatory state" (Alma 12:26), it's nonetheless also true that this preparatory state is what defines our mortal condition as "lost and . . . fallen" (v. 22). The logic, here, is straightforward. Fallen, we gain agency. As agents, we itch to act. Always itching to act and do something else, life itself becomes a preparatory state.

Always preparing for something other than the lives we're presently living, we experience—in the middle of life itself—a kind of death. Even before we die our first death, we experience a second death. This second death results from living our lives in a suspended, preparatory state. That is, this second death, creeping into life's own bones, results from living our lives preparing, as Alma says, for death and judgment. Always looking forward, always preparing for death and judgment, our lives get defined by the ends that are coming. Anticipating death and judgment, we live our lives under the sign of death, conditioned by death, measuring each thing with an eye of judgment as it passes our way. Conditioned by death and judgment, the present gets lived in the future, and, as a result, we become alienated from the present.

Living our lives in this fallen, preparatory state, we may lose our bearings and become convinced that redemption is what comes *after* death and judgment. Redemption starts to look like something that comes *after* we have exercised our agency and demonstrated obedience. But, always looking forward to redemption as a future outcome, as an effect that we by our agency must in some way cause, we then find it impossible to "enter into the rest of God" here and now (Alma 12:37).

As with the Israelites, God's wrath is provoked by this refusal to enter the promised land and find that rest. The Israelites, led by Moses out of Egypt and to the brink of the promised land, balk at reports of the strength of the opposition and turn back (cf. Numbers 13:1–14:20).

In response, God condemns them to wander, lost, for forty years in the wilderness, until death has claimed them. This, I think, is a model for human fallenness. Fallenness is this refusal to enter God's rest here and now, this insistence on postponing redemption until after death, this failure to accept the redemption that is already prepared and given from the foundation of the world, this attachment to living life as preparation for something other than life.

A preparatory redemption

However, on Alma's account, redemption is not what comes after commandments and obedience. Redemption is not what comes after death. Rather, as Alma repeatedly insists, the plan of redemption was, instead, prepared "from the foundation of the world."

This, really, is my only point: there appears to be a big difference between living our lives in "a preparatory state" and entering into what Alma calls "a preparatory redemption." It is important to avoid confusing the one with the other. The first (a preparatory state) defines our fallen condition, the second (a preparatory redemption) defines the character of our redemption. Lost and fallen, people are forever preparing for a redemption that, in Christ, has already been prepared. In fact, it has been prepared from the foundation of the world.

What, though, does it mean for something to be prepared "from the foundation of the world"? Initially, Alma uses this formula to describe what he calls "the plan of redemption." In Alma 12:25, he refers to "the plan of redemption which was laid from the foundation of the world." In verses 25 and 33, Alma also uses abbreviated versions of this formula and refers to "a plan of redemption laid" and "the plan of redemption which was laid." Then, in verse 30, with a slight modification, he refers to "the plan of redemption which had been prepared from the foundation of the world."

The plan of redemption is primordial. It is not a backup plan. It is not an ad hoc response to Adam and Eve's transgression in Eden or to human sinfulness in general. On this account, the plan of redemption is what comes *first*. As Revelation 13:8 puts it, Christ is himself the "Lamb slain from the foundation of the world." In defiance of expectation and chronology, the plan of redemption comes first; being lost and fallen always and only comes second.

Alma makes this same point in connection with God's commandments. On Alma's telling in 12:32, "God gave unto them commandments *after* having made known unto them the plan of redemption." Here, God gives several sets of commandments: both the first commandments given in the garden (v. 31) and a second set of commandments "that they should not do evil" once humans have left the garden (v. 32). But the plan of redemption, already prepared from the foundation of the world, is "made known unto them" *before* this second set of commandments is given. The commandments, as given to us, are not identical to the plan of redemption—otherwise they couldn't have been given after the plan had already been made known. And the commandments, unlike the plan, are never described as being from the foundation of the world.

Clearly, the commandments bear some relation to redemption, but, as Paul insists, the priority of God's redemptive grace forces us to "conclude that a man is justified by faith without the deeds of the law" (Romans 3:28). What, then, of the law? "Do we then make void the law through faith? God forbid: yea, we establish the law" (v. 31). While the law clearly cannot redeem, it can still be rightly said that the plan of redemption does itself both give and fulfill the law.

As Paul puts it, the key to entering, here and now, into the rest of God is faith in Christ. Or, returning to Alma's language, the key to entering into God's rest is, Alma says, a certain "manner" of "looking forward" to Christ. This redemptive manner of looking forward will need to be clearly distinguished, however, from the kind of looking forward that defines our fallen experience as a preparatory state. What distinguishes this redemptive "manner" of looking forward to Christ from our typical fallen manner of looking forward to death and judgment?

The holy order of God

While Alma initially describes the plan of redemption as being prepared from the foundation of the world, he also uses this same formula to describe what he calls "the holy order of God" (Alma 13:6). By pairing both with the foundation of the world, Alma indicates that the plan of redemption is, in some crucial way, synonymous with the holy order of God.

In Alma 13:3, priests of this holy order are "called and prepared from the foundation of the world." In verse 5, the "holy calling" (rather than priests) is described as "being prepared from the foundation of the world." And in verse 7, the order itself, "this high priesthood being after the order of his Son," is described as being "from the foundation of the world."

More, this holy order, prepared from the foundation of the world, opens onto what Alma calls "a preparatory redemption" (Alma 13:3). Entering into this preparatory redemption, one can enter into the rest of God. Instead of endlessly preparing, one can rest (even while acting) because, unlike living in a preparatory state—that is, in a state of perpetually preparing *for* death and judgment—this preparatory redemption has *already* been prepared from the foundation of the world by the Son himself.

All of this comes back to Alma's use of the formula "from the foundation of the world." In 13:7, Alma appends an explicit explanation to his use of that phrase:

> this high priesthood being after the order of his Son, which order was from the foundation of the world, *or in other words*, being without beginning of days or end of years, being prepared from eternity to all eternity according to his foreknowledge of all things.

With this gloss, Alma 13:7 offers an especially significant example of the sermon's more or less continuous appropriation and transformation of a constellation of formulas native to the biblical book of Hebrews. This language clusters around the figure of Melchizedek (see Alma 13:14–19) but tracks across the whole of Hebrews 3, 4, and 7.

In this instance, the proximate parallel for the language about "the foundation of the world" is Hebrews 4:3: "For we who have believed enter that rest, as he has said, 'As I swore in my anger, "They will never enter my rest!'" And yet God's works were accomplished from the foundation of the world" (New English Translation). In this verse from Hebrews 4, "God's works" are described as having been finished from the foundation of the world. The works in question are the work of creating or "founding" the world itself. Upon completing the work of founding the world, God then "rested" on the seventh day. This already completed work is the central issue, both for the author of Hebrews and for Alma: both are concerned with what it means to finish one's work and "enter into the rest of the Lord" (Alma 12:37; cf. 12:34–36; 13:6, 12, 13, 16), and this rest is exemplified by the Sabbath into which God enters following the work of creation. Those "who have believed enter that rest" and share in this sabbatical way of life, while, on the other hand, those who fail to look forward to the Son in this manner wander, lost and fallen, in the wilderness, continually preparing for death and judgment.

Alma, though, in the process of adapting this language, changes the meaning of the formula. In 13:7, he joins this passage in Hebrews 4:3 with language proper to Hebrews 7:3, a verse that describes Melchizedek himself as being "without father, without mother, without descent, having neither beginning of days, nor end of life; but made like unto the Son of God; abideth a priest continually." Alma detaches this description from the person of Melchizedek, attaches it to the holy order itself, and then rereads the "foundation of the world" as meaning something that is "without beginning of days or end of years."

Where Hebrews 4:3 uses "foundation of the world" to refer to the seven days of God's work of creating or founding the world, Alma instead uses this formula to refer to something that defies mortal chronology and has no beginning of days or end of years. This is to say, where Hebrews reads "foundation of the world" as a reference to God's past tense and completed act of creation, Alma takes up this language of creating the world and then suggests that this work of creating or founding the world is itself eternal. This work is, in fact, present tense and ongoing. "Being prepared from eternity to all eternity," the work of creation is being eternally prepared. The work of creating and re-creating the world is eternal. As King Benjamin puts it, God not only created the world, but he *continually* creates the world by "preserving" and "supporting" it "from one moment to another" (Mosiah 2:21).

This is an important point. *When* is the creation of the world? I'm suggesting that the foundation of the world is *now*. God not only founded the world in the past—he's founding the world right now, from moment to moment. And if the plan of redemption is itself prepared from the foundation of the world, then when is redemption available? Redemption is available now.

A certain "manner" of looking forward

But how is this possible? How would one enter into this rest in the present rather than aiming for it in the future or, alternately, longing for it as something lost, deep in the past? How is it possible for creation and redemption to defy mortal chronology? This way of experiencing time and life as redeemed rather than probationary depends, as Alma indicated, on a certain "manner" of looking forward to Christ. This manner is, in short, a certain posture that, in faith, can be adopted in relation to time.

In 13:16, Alma puts it like this: "Now these ordinances were given after this manner, that thereby the people might look forward on the Son of God, it being a type of his order or it being his order—and this that they might look forward to him for a remission of their sins, that they might enter into the rest of the Lord." Note that, though the ordinances (i.e., the laws or rituals) are important, in the end they are not the point. Rather, what's at stake here is not the ordinances themselves but the *manner* after which they were given.

This same point is emphasized especially in Alma 13:2. There, Alma says, "those priests were ordained after the order of his Son in a manner that thereby the people might know in what manner to look forward to his Son for redemption." The priests are ordained "in a manner" that will display for the people something crucial about "in what manner to look forward" to the Son. The same formula is used again in verse 3 ("and this is the manner") and in verse 8 ("now they were ordained after this manner"). However, as verse 16 emphasizes, it's not the ordinance itself (as a noun) or even the ordaining (as a verb) that's ultimately at stake. Rather, it's the *manner* (as an adverb) of the ordaining that is crucial. Adverbs aren't the subject or the action, but a certain mode or manner of both. Adverbs modify verbs. It seems to me that redemption, here, is ultimately adverbial. In the grammar of Alma's soteriology, redemption is not a noun or a verb but an adverb.

Etymologically, the word *manner* comes from the Latin word *manus* or hand. That is, a manner is a certain way of "handling" something. In the context of our verses, this manner hinges, I think, on a certain way of "handling" time. For usage in Joseph Smith's day, the 1828 Webster's dictionary gives the following range of meanings: form, method, way of performing or executing; custom or habitual practice; sort or kind; certain degree or measure; mien, cast of look, or mode; a peculiar way or carriage.

The King James Bible frequently uses the word *manner*. Some instances of its use are helpful, though, and some are not. One useful example is 1 Kings 22:20. This verse describes various plans for persuading Ahab, and we're told that "one said on this manner, and another said on that manner." Here, the Hebrew word rendered as "manner" is *koh* and means something like: properly, like this, thus, here, so, in this manner. What is a manner? It's doing something "thus."

Another example: in 2 Kings 17:26, those that "know not the manner of the God of the land" are devoured by an army of lions. Here, the Hebrew word rendered as "manner" is *mishpat*, a word that, basically, has to do with judgment but covers a range of meanings like: what is just, proper, fitting, and then by extension a custom or habitual manner of doing something.

This, then, runs up against our English usage of *manners* to describe the proper or fitting way to habitually act, like having dinner manners. Manner, in this sense, is a fitting habit, a habitual way of acting that is in tune with its context. It intersects with the notion of *habitus*, in an Aristotelian sense, as a structured potential.

Two more examples. In the New Testament, in Luke 1:29, Mary, troubled by the angel's visit, "cast in her mind what manner of salutation this should be." Here, the Greek word rendered as "manner" is *potapos* and means something like "from what country or tribe is this?" or, by extension, "of what sort or quality is this thing?"

In a final example, in John 2:6, we're told that there were six water pots of stone "after the manner of the purifying of the Jews." Here the Greek word for "manner" is just the generic preposition *kata* and basically means something like "according to." Things acquire a manner, a modulated character, when they are not just performed but performed "according to" a certain pattern.

This, then, is what is at stake in this redemptive manner of looking forward to Christ: a certain way "handling" time, a certain kind of quality, a way of being "thus," a habitual style of acting that is in tune with its context, or a particular "mode" that acts according to a pattern. In sum, manners are, fundamentally, adverbial.

As an adverb, this manner of ordination exemplifies, on Alma's account, the proper manner of looking forward. And, in addition, we're told in Alma 13:16 that this manner of looking has explicitly to do with the manner in which the ordinances "were given." This manner of looking is a manner of giving. This connection between "looking" and "giving" may also be what prompts Alma's return to the question of this manner in verse 16 immediately following his description of how "our father Abraham paid tithes of one tenth part of all he possessed" to Melchizedek (v. 15).

"These ordinances" in Alma 13:16 may refer, in part, to the ritual of giving a consecrated tithe. Or, at the very least, we might see these priestly ordinations as themselves being an exemplary case of a consecrated tithe: instead of giving a tithe on one's property, ordination offers up the whole of the priest's life as an act of consecration. This manner of giving displays the proper manner of looking forward, a way of looking forward that isn't fallen: it is a kind of looking forward that, by way of consecration, dispossesses itself of itself for the sake of the Son. It is a way of looking forward that gives itself up.

However, apart from this rich context, Alma 13:16 also gives an explicit description of this manner of looking forward. This manner of looking forward is typological: "These ordinances were given after this manner, that thereby the people might look forward on the Son of God, it being a type of his order."

Types of Christ

What is a type? The idea is biblical, though the King James Version does not itself use the word *type*. Rather, in key instances such as Romans 5:14, it instead translates the Greek word *tupos* as "figure," describing Adam as "the figure of him that was to come." *Tupos* literally means the mark or stroke of a blow, or the imprint left by that blow. By extension it means a figure or an image, a teaching that condenses a complex set of ideas, a pattern in conformity with which a thing must be made, an example, or something that prefigures something else.

The most salient meaning for our purposes is the last: a type is something that prefigures something else. That is, a type is a figure that allows for something to appear out of chronological order and arrive before its expected time. This redemptive manner of looking forward, as typological, depends on looking at things to come as having already arrived. Though the Lamb of God is not yet slain, he is, nonetheless, slain from the foundation of the world. And when is the foundation of the world? As I indicated earlier, the foundation of the world is always *now*.

The Book of Mormon's clearest description of this typological manner of looking forward is given in Jarom 1:11: "The prophets and the priests and the teachers did labor diligently, exhorting with all long-suffering the people to diligence, . . . persuading them to look forward unto the Messiah and believe in him to come as though he already was. And after this manner did they teach them." Here we've got all the key terms: *priests*, *manner*, and *looking forward*, though instead of using the word *type*, we get a description of what it *means* to look at something typologically. To look forward to the Son typologically is to "believe in him to come as though he already was."

This, then, is the manner of looking forward. It is a typological manner, a manner that holds time in a certain way and that, in doing so, consecrates our looking forward and gives back what is looked forward to, in order to see the truth: that what *can* be looked forward to is already being given now.

Rather than living in a preparatory state, rather living the present only in light of its hope for the future, this typologically modified experience of time enters into the rest of a redemption already prepared from the foundation of the world, and, as a result, it lives the future as already given and created in the present.

In this sense, the typological ordinance par excellence is baptism. The manner of baptism exemplifies in what manner one should look forward to Christ. By way of baptism, the participant dies early. They die *before* their bodies have failed. By way of baptism, they stop preparing for death and just get death over with.

Dying before their time, they give up their own lives and, instead, take up what Paul calls "life in Christ" (Romans 8:2). Then, no longer preparing for death and judgment—they are already dead after all—they can enter into that rest that has already, from the foundation of the world, been prepared. "Know ye not, that so many of us as were baptized into Jesus Christ were baptized into his death? Therefore we are buried with him by baptism into death: that like as Christ was raised up from the dead by the glory of the Father, even so we also should walk in newness of life" (Romans 6:3–4).

Conclusion

Life in Christ is structured in this manner as a type, and these ordinances, Alma says, are given in such a way as to exemplify this manner of living time. Rather than living the present in the future, this manner lives the future in the present. Or, we might say: living time in this manner, the Christian no longer lives life as a way of preparing for death. Rather, like Christ, they live death itself as just one part of life.

Called and Ordained: A Priesthood of All Believers in Alma 13

Bridget Jack Jeffries

Mormon theology as an "inside-outsider"

Theology is, by definition, the study of who God is. But as a member of the Evangelical Covenant Church, I would answer the question of who God is differently than most Latter-day Saints would. As a result, in relation to the LDS tradition, I am what Jan Shipps called an "inside-outsider."[1] I'm deeply familiar with Mormon ideas and practices, but my own faith and commitments lie elsewhere. However, even when people disagree on fundamental theological questions, dialogue can still be a productive and important part of our shared commitment to the work of thinking about God.

In this spirit, think of the essay that follows as an experiment. What happens when an evangelical Christian devotes herself to the work of reading a rich and challenging selection from the Book of Mormon? In particular, how might Alma's account of priesthood in Alma 13 be differently understood if, instead of assuming a contemporary LDS understanding of priesthood as its defining backdrop, the text is read with fresh eyes from an evangelical perspective? What areas of

1. See Jan Shipps, "An 'Inside-Outsider' in Zion," *Dialogue* 15/1 (1982): 138–61.

common agreement might emerge, and what differences may be more clearly defined?

The question of priesthood

To begin, allow me to sketch some of the assumptions that frame my own approach to the topic of priesthood. Priesthood models vary widely between denominations. Biblically, the Levitical priesthood (Exodus 28:41) restricted priesthood to the sons of Aaron, within the tribe of Levi, within the people of Israel, meaning that only a very small portion of human beings were eligible to serve as priests. Within this already restricted priestly group, only one man could serve as high priest over the people (Leviticus 16:30–34). Modern-day iterations of priesthood vary greatly. Roman Catholics, for example, restrict their priesthood to males who pledge to live a celibate life, while Latter-day Saints make theirs available to all males over the age of twelve, whether married or single. Protestants subscribe to a more open system of priesthood, teaching a "priesthood of all believers" wherein every member is a priest and thus able to approach the "throne of grace with confidence" (Hebrews 4:16 NIV). However, within this framework, it is important to distinguish between the issue of priesthood in general and the question of formal ordination as clergy. While priesthood and clerical ordination are synonymous in Roman Catholic and Eastern Orthodox thought, and are almost inseparably intertwined in LDS thought, the two are distinct in Protestant thought. For Protestants, all believers are recognized as holding a priesthood of sorts, but not all believers are ordained as clergy. In what follows, I will treat only the concept of priesthood itself and leave aside the more nuanced question of sacerdotal ordination.

If, then, we work only from the details of the Book of Mormon text itself, which of these models, if any, does the priesthood described in Alma 13 most closely resemble?

The function of priests in Alma 13

As described in Alma 13, the function of the priests is more evangelistic than sacerdotal. In his response to Antionah, Alma first mentions priesthood when he urges his audience to "remember that the Lord God ordained priests after his holy order, which was after the order of his Son, to teach these things unto the people" (Alma 13:1). Here, the distinguishing feature of priesthood is not the administration of salvific ordinances but the work of teaching "these things" to the people, and by "these things" Alma means the gospel as laid out in the previous chapter: the fall from Eden (Alma 12:21–24), a plan of redemption (v. 25), the way of salvation (vv. 33–34, 37), temporal death (v. 27), the resurrection of the dead (v. 20), and the fate of the damned (vv. 35–36). To teach such things to others and thus facilitate their salvation is, as Alma describes it, the essence of being a priest "after the order of [the] Son" (Alma 13:1).

In connection with this basic function, Alma notes that these priests were ordained so that "the people might know in what manner to look forward to [God's] Son for redemption" (Alma 13:2) and that they were chosen "on account of their exceeding faith and good works" (v. 3) rather than on account of external factors like lineage or race. In this respect, Alma's priests do not appear to be Levitical or attached to the temple cult. While ancient Israel had only one "high priest" (cf. Leviticus 16:30–34), Alma is clear that in this case "there were many which were ordained and became high priests of God" (v. 10). Apart from the mention of ordination itself, Alma 13 never ties the work of these priests to the ecclesiastical business of offering salvific ordinances or even to the work of administering ritual sacrifices as required by the law of Moses. Rather, the functions performed by these priests—namely, to teach the people "in what manner to look forward to [God's] Son for redemption" and "to teach his commandments unto the children of men" (vv. 3, 6)—are responsibilities that appear to be shared by all believers in Christ.

Calling and foreordination

In a similar way, the qualifications of these priests—faith, good works, choosing what is good—are qualifications to which all believers should aspire. Alma 13 repeatedly notes that Alma's priests were "called and prepared from the foundation of the world" and that they were "called with a holy calling" (see 13:3–8). The text further declares that these priests were called and prepared "according to the foreknowledge of God, on account of their exceeding faith and good works—in the first place being left to choose good or evil" (v. 3).[2] In contrast, others are not called "to this holy calling" because God foreknew that they would "reject the Spirit of God on account of the hardness of their hearts and blindness of their minds—while if it had not been for this, they might [have] had as great privilege as their brethren" (v. 4).

Alma also goes out of his way to argue that there was nothing unfair about these priesthood callings. Of those who were *not* called, Alma says: "In the first place they were on the same standing with their brethren" who *were* called (Alma 13:5). Those who were not called as priests had the same opportunity to be called as those who were, but they were not called because God foreknew that they "would reject the Spirit of God" (v. 4).

In this respect, Alma's description of the calling and election of these priests resonates with the theology of Jacobus Arminius, whose alternative to Calvinism held that God's foreordination, calling, and choosing of the elect was based on his foreknowledge of who would choose him. Working from this premise, we might also read the mention of "preparatory redemption" in Alma 13:3 as a nod to the Arminian concept of "prevenient grace," where God preemptively liberated humanity from the "total depravity" of original sin and

---

2. While this reference to "the first place" is sometimes read as an invocation of the LDS doctrine of premortal existence, this does not appear to be the most natural reading. While Alma never explicitly mentions a doctrine of premortal existence—in fact, no Book of Mormon authors do—he does clearly frame these priestly callings in Alma 13 in terms of God's *foreknowledge*.

enabled humankind to choose his salvation.[3] Alma's priests have been empowered from the foundation of the world to choose both good and evil, and their calling and ordination is based on God's foreknowledge of what they would eventually choose.

If this reading is viable, then Alma 13 may largely align with the Methodist theology of John Wesley, who popularized Arminianism in the Protestant world and whose teachings were known to Joseph Smith (see, for example, JS—H 1:5). In opposition to the "irresistible grace" of Calvinism, Wesley believed in a God who allowed human beings to freely choose salvation. He asked: "How is it more for the glory of God to save man irresistibly, than to save him as a free agent, by such grace as he may either concur or resist?"[4] Wesley also taught:

> Yea, the decree is past; and so it was before the foundation of the world. But what decree? Even this: "I will set before the sons of men 'life and death, blessing cursing.' And the soul that chooseth life shall live, as the soul that chooseth death shall die." This decree whereby "whom God did foreknow, he did predestinate," was indeed from everlasting; this, whereby all who suffer Christ to make them alive are "elect according to the foreknowledge of God," now standeth fast, even as the moon, and as the faithful witnesses in heaven; and when heaven and earth shall pass away, yet this shall not pass away; for it is as unchangeable and eternal as is the being of God that gave it. This decree yields the strongest encouragement to abound in all good works and in all holiness; and it is a well-spring of joy, of happiness also, to our great and endless comfort. This is worthy of God; it is every way

---

3. For a basic assessment of prevenient grace, see Millard J. Erickson, *Christian Theology*, 2nd ed. (Grand Rapids: Baker Academic, 1998), 932–33.

4. John Wesley, "Predestination Calmly Considered," in *The Complete Works of John Wesley: Vol. 10, Letters, Essays, Dialogs, and Addresses* (Albany, OR: Books for the Ages, 1997), 272.

> consistent with all the perfections of his nature. It gives us the noblest view both of his justice, mercy, and truth.[5]

Wesley's teachings appear to harmonize with the words of Alma. Both Alma's priests and Wesley's believers are called with a calling that is from "the foundation of the world" (Alma 13:3, 7). Both are able to choose "life and death, blessing cursing" (Wesley) or "good or evil" (v. 3). Both are called "according to [God's] foreknowledge of all things" and are part of an order that is "eternal" and "shall not pass away" (Wesley), "being without beginning of days or end of years, being prepared from eternity to all eternity" (v. 7). The parallels between the two are striking. In my view, Alma 13 might best be read as an Arminian soteriology that has then been creatively fused with a doctrine of priesthood.[6]

However, this hypothesis comes with a significant caveat. This fusion of priesthood with an Arminian soteriology only makes good sense if the priesthood of Alma 13 is available to all believers. If priesthood and salvation are this tightly intertwined, then priesthood, like salvation, would have to be available to everyone, regardless of their lineage, race, or even gender. When one views the priesthood and holy calling of Alma 13 not as something exclusive and limited, but as something that is available to an "exceedingly great many" (13:12)—that is, to *all* who would choose good over evil—then these pieces fit together seamlessly.

The risk of priestly privilege: The making of nonpriests

As mentioned previously, Alma 13:4 seems particularly concerned with establishing that there has been no unfair treatment of nonpriests. Alma wants to assure his listeners that there are no unjustified inequalities

5. John Wesley, "Free Grace," Sermon 128:29, in *The Sermons of John Wesley*, ed. Ken Harris, with the assistance of Ryan Danker and George Lyons (Nampa, ID: Wesley Center for Applied Theology, 1999), http://bit.ly/22oX1nt.

6. For more on the similarities between LDS and Wesleyan thought, see Christopher C. Jones, "We Latter-day Saints Are Methodists: The Influence of Methodism on Early Mormon Religiosity" (master's thesis, Brigham Young University, 2009).

between the two groups, and he takes great pains to establish that the calling of the priestly group can be traced to God's foreknowledge of their "exceeding faith and good works" (v. 3), while nonpriests "would reject the Spirit of God on account of the hardness of their hearts and blindness of their minds" (v. 4). He continues, "if it had not been for this [the nonpriests] might [have] had as great privilege as their brethren" (v. 4). And, again, he argues that "in the first place [the nonpriests] were on the same standing with their [priestly] brethren" (v. 5).[7] In all this, the author is keen to show that God "is no respecter of persons" (Acts 10:34) and that all had an opportunity to ascend to this priesthood.

In this respect, the advantage of the Protestant doctrine of a "priesthood of all believers" is obvious because it comports so thoroughly with the Christian intuition that God is no respecter of persons. In a priesthood of all believers, no one is excluded from this holy calling except for those who have chosen to exclude themselves. In contrast, the weakness of modern priesthood systems that exclude participation on the basis of lineage, race, or gender is also clear: whole classes of people are excluded from God's holy calling for reasons that are not linked to their faithfulness. The trouble with creating an exclusive priestly class is that it unavoidably and automatically creates a class of nonpriests. Alma is clearly concerned with the possibility that this division may be perceived as unfair, and so he grounds the distinction entirely in worthiness. But when the distinction between priests and nonpriests is made on other grounds, like race or lineage, then the concern that originally motivated Alma's own explanation is left unaddressed.

Historically, the concern raised in Alma 13:4 has been broadly justified. In order to explain why whole classes of people have been excluded from the priesthood, these classes have been consistently slandered. Highly negative theories have circulated about the groups in question. In LDS history, for instance, the now-discarded theory that blacks of African descent were less valiant in the premortal existence is one example of a theory that places the blame for nonordination

7. I believe that this portion of Alma 13:5 would be better punctuated and grouped with verse 4, with verse 5 beginning with, "Thus this holy calling being prepared . . ."

on the actions of an entire race. And, in broader Christian history, early church fathers and other Christian leaders had regularly taught that women should not be ordained because, as a whole, women were naturally more susceptible to sin than men. While many Christian denominations have repudiated the idea that women are inherently more sinful than men, and while the contemporary LDS Church has emphatically stated that it "disavows the theories advanced in the past that black skin is a sign of divine disfavor or curse, or that it reflects unrighteous actions in a premortal life; that mixed-race marriages are a sin; or that blacks or people of any other race or ethnicity are inferior in any way to anyone else,"[8] it seems to me that the practice of excluding certain classes of people from the possibility of priesthood ordination still carries substantial risks. It is to the Book of Mormon's immense credit that, in its only sustained discussion of priesthood (see Alma 13:1–20), the text is so sensitive to these risks.

Possible objections to reading Alma 13 as invoking a priesthood of all believers

As provocative as the resonances may be between Alma's treatment of priesthood in Alma 13 and the Protestant doctrine of a priesthood of all believers, some loose ends remain.

It might be observed, for instance, that the language of Alma's sermon is almost entirely gendered. He repeatedly refers to his audience as his "brethren" (see, for example, Alma 12:36, 37; 13:1, 13), thereby suggesting either that the author only has men in mind for identification with these "priests" or that only men were visualized as being present in the group listening to the sermon. While this objection is significant, it does not appear to me to be decisive. (And, even if we grant the point, it would only move the larger problem back one level: if women are excluded from Alma's audience outright, all the acknowledged risks that follow from excluding entire classes of people from the priesthood still remain.) The use of the term *brethren* is not decisive

8. "Race and the Priesthood," The Church of Jesus Christ of Latter-day Saints, December 2013, https://www.lds.org/topics/race-and-the-priesthood?lang=eng.

in itself with respect to the composition of Alma's audience because the masculine plural is potentially gender inclusive in most gendered languages. Either all of the Book of Mormon's sermons aimed at brethren are intended for men only, or it is up to the reader to determine where *brethren* is meant to function as an inclusive masculine plural in particular cases. In the case of Alma 13, there is some indication that women were present among the listeners of the sermon. Alma 14:8 states that "whosoever believed or had been taught to believe in the word of God" as a result of Alma's preaching—including "wives and children"—were "cast into the fire." As such, it is possible that women were included in the group addressed in Alma 13. Though, given that this mass execution of women and children did not take place immediately after Alma's sermon, it is also possible that women were not present at the sermon itself but, instead, received the message secondhand from the men of their households.

Another objection might be that the members of Alma's priestly group are said to be "ordained with a holy ordinance" (Alma 13:8), and this suggestion of a literal ordination might fit poorly with the doctrine of a priesthood of all believers. Yet this particular problem is not without precedent. Martin Luther addressed this same difficulty when he argued in 1520 for a biblical foundation to the doctrine of a universal priesthood. In his "Open Letter to the Christian Nobility of the German Nation," Luther explained:

> But that a pope or a bishop anoints, confers tonsures; ordains, consecrates, or prescribes dress unlike that of the laity,—this may make hypocrites and graven images, but it never makes a Christian or "spiritual" man. Through baptism all of us are consecrated to the priesthood, as St. Peter says in I Peter ii, "Ye are a royal priesthood, a priestly kingdom," and the book of Revelation says, "Thou hast made us by Thy blood to be priests and kings."[9]

9. Martin Luther, "An Open Letter to the Christian Nobility of the German Nation Concerning the Reform of the Christian Estate," 1520; 1915 Charles Michael Jacobs translation, 66. Luther quotes from 1 Peter 2:9 and Revelation 5:10, respectively.

Later that same year, Luther maintained that "all of us that have been baptized are equally priests."[10] From this point of view, it may be possible to argue that the ritual of ordination in question in passages such as Alma 13:8 could be baptism itself rather than the laying on of hands. The text itself is vague. Doubtless, a reading of Alma 13 that assumes contemporary LDS teachings about priesthood as its frame will not find this suggestion especially persuasive. But if this contemporary LDS framework is not taken as the starting point for interpreting Alma 13, then I believe a variety of alternate readings—including my own—may not only be possible but persuasive.

Conclusion: Room for agreement?

I have read the text of Alma 13 with Protestant eyes and interpreted it in a Protestant light, understanding it with the aid of similar texts by Protestant theologians. But does the Protestant nature of my interpretation of Alma 13 require Mormons to reject it out of hand? Is there any room for agreement between our respective movements?

I think that there is. My LDS friends often express solidarity with the Roman Catholic priesthood over the Protestant model of a priesthood of believers because the former claims an unbroken line of authority from the apostles of Jesus Christ up through the current pope, as do Mormons with their current prophet. Ordination by a laying on of hands is required by both, and, officially, only males may hold either of these priesthoods. Given these similarities, I find it understandable that many Mormons gravitate toward Roman Catholicism as Mormonism's closest priesthood analog.[11]

However, the Mormon priesthood is very different from the Roman Catholic priesthood in one regard: the Roman Catholic priesthood is highly restrictive. Apart from some few exceptions, only celibate males may hold it. The vast majority of Roman Catholics, male or female, are

---

10. Martin Luther, *The Babylonian Captivity of the Church, 1520: The Annotated Luther Study Edition*, with contributions by Erik H. Herrmann, ed. Paul W. Robinson (Minneapolis, MN: Fortress Press, 2016), 115.

11. Although the Eastern Orthodox system of priesthood would work just as well.

not priests and do not claim to be. It cannot be considered a "priesthood of believers" in any meaningful sense.

In contrast, the Mormon priesthood is held by nearly half the members of the church ages twelve and up. The only group excluded is women—and several LDS leaders have indicated that LDS women *do* hold the priesthood in some enigmatic way. For example, though he did not formally ordain women, Brigham Young taught, "The man that honors his Priesthood, the woman that honors *her Priesthood*, will receive an everlasting inheritance in the kingdom of God."[12] As such, rather than thinking of LDS priesthood as an analog for Roman Catholic priesthood, it may be useful to think of it as a hybrid of Roman Catholicism's male-only, restrictive, linear priesthood, and Protestantism's priesthood of all believers. It has aspects of both.

It is in this light that I believe Mormons may begin looking for theological similarities between my interpretation of Alma 13 and their own. May we ever be seeking greater understanding of one another, regardless.

12. Brigham Young, in *Journal of Discourses* 17:119 (28 June 1874), emphasis added.

Contributors

MATTHEW BOWMAN is associate professor of history at Henderson State University and author of *The Mormon People: The Making of an American Faith* (Random House, 2012), *The Urban Pulpit: New York City and the Fate of Liberal Evangelicalism* (Oxford, 2014), and the most significant study of Mormon Bigfoot folklore yet published.

ROSEMARY DEMOS has a PhD in comparative literature from the City University of New York Graduate Center. She teaches in the English Department at Hunter College. Her research and writing focus on religion in literature.

DAVID CHARLES GORE is associate professor and chair in the Department of Communication at the University of Minnesota Duluth. He teaches courses in the history of rhetoric and publishes in the rhetoric of economics, rhetorical theory, and Mormon studies.

BRIDGET JACK JEFFRIES is an independent scholar from Chicago with an MA in American religious history from Trinity Evangelical Divinity School. She is the author of *Mormongelical: An Interfaith Memoir* (forthcoming), and her interviews on religion have appeared in *The Washington Post* and *Religion & Ethics Newsweekly.*

Adam S. Miller is Honors Institute Director and a professor of philosophy at Collin College in McKinney, Texas. He is the author of seven books, including *Speculative Grace*, *The Gospel According to David Foster Wallace*, and *Future Mormon*. He is the director of the Mormon Theology Seminar and coedits, with Joseph Spencer, a series of books for the Maxwell Institute called Groundwork: Studies in Theory and Scripture.

Robert A. Rees teaches and is the director of Mormon studies at Graduate Theological Union in Berkeley. Previously, he taught literature and humanities at UCLA and UC Santa Cruz and was a Fulbright Professor of American Studies in the Baltics. He has published a number of books, essays, and articles on Mormonism, including *The Reader's Book of Mormon* (with Eugene England), *Why I Stay: The Challenges of Discipleship for Contemporary Mormons*, and *Proving Contraries: A Collection of Writings in Honor of Eugene England*. His collection of poems, *Waiting for Morning*, was published in 2017.

Joseph M. Spencer is visiting assistant professor of ancient scripture at Brigham Young University. He's the author of many articles and three books, most recently *The Vision of All: Twenty-Five Lectures on Isaiah in Nephi's Record* (Greg Kofford Books, 2016). He is the editor of the *Journal of Book of Mormon Studies* and serves as the associate director of the Mormon Theology Seminar. He and Karen, his wife, live in Provo, Utah, with their five children.

Sheila Taylor has a PhD in systematic theology from the Graduate Theological Union. She has published on salvation and feminist theology and is currently editing a volume on Mormon perspectives on grace. She lives in Bloomington, Indiana.